CW01023003

ISBN 978-1-331-39001-5
PIBN 10183457

FB &c Ltd, Dalton House, 60 Windsor Avenue, London, SW19 2RR.
Company number 08720141. Registered in England and Wales.

For support please visit www.forgottenbooks.com

IMITATIONS AND TRANSLATIONS,

TOGETHER WITH

ORIGINAL POEMS.

T. Davison, Whitefriars,
London.

IMITATIONS AND TRANSLATIONS

FROM THE

ANCIENT AND MODERN CLASSICS,

TOGETHER WITH

ORIGINAL POEMS

NEVER BEFORE PUBLISHED.

COLLLECTED BY

J. C. HOBHOUSE, B. A.

OF

TRINITY COLLEGE, CAMBRIDGE.

" Nos hæc novimus esse nihil."

LONDON:

PRINTED FOR LONGMAN, HURST, REES, AND ORME,

PATERNOSTER-ROW.

1809.

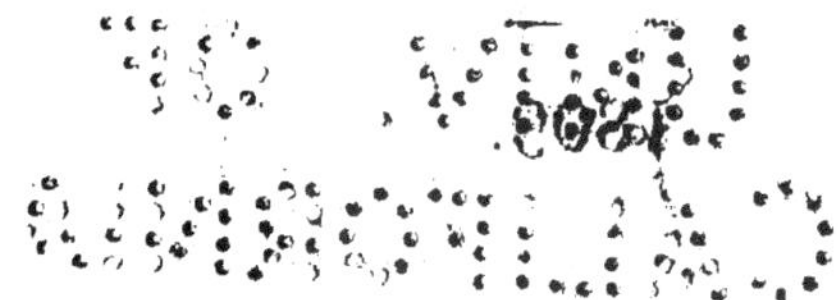

It should seem that the world at present suffers from a glut of books; but notwithstanding every person appears impressed with this notion, I know scarcely any one amongst my acquaintance who has not occasionally felt a desire, and that a very strong one, to venture at publication. It is not, however, very difficult to account for the prevalence of this propensity, for the multitude of writings on every subject, which characterises the times, and which might be supposed to deter an author from increasing a number already too large, is doubtless one of the causes which operate to make so many candidates for literary reputation; for each man considers, that if he fail in his pursuit, he will have many partners in his disgrace; and if he attain his object, he must become the more conspicuous by his triumph over a multitude of unsuccessful rivals. It must, however, be acknowledged, that if writers are unreasonably numerous, they are all sufficiently ready to confess their incapacity; for it is curious to observe the various excuses, deprecations, and confessions contained in modern prefaces. And here I do not allude only to the works of the present day; for if we may believe the professions of the wits who distinguished the English Augustan age at the beginning of the last century, we must consider even these, for the most part, equally aware of the blame which they might incur by commencing authors, equally willing to plead for their presumption, and to offer some cause and reason for appearing before the public *at such a time and under such circumstances.*

One, "can no longer withstand the repeated solicitations of his friends." Another "has incautiously suffered too many copies of his compositions to get about, and must therefore print in his own vindication to prevent a surreptitious and incorrect edition." A third "has written most of his pieces when very young; and being unwilling to deceive the public into a false opinion of his early prowess by the corrections of his mature judgment, has e'en sent them into the world just as they were originally produced, and therefore trusts he shall meet with every indulgence." We find many "who have given much time and consideration to the subject before them, but who are as likely as any in the world to be mistaken; yet hope that what was performed with care will not be criticised in haste." This gentleman has been maliciously reported to be the author of some scurrilous lampoons and indecent poems; and therefore to shew how incapable he is of such an impropriety, and how little his mind has ever taken such a turn, boldly gives to the world FIVE SATIRES and A TALE FROM BOCCACE. We generally see that Poems "were written for the amusement of a leisure hour, and are therefore unfit subjects for ill-natured censure." Political and religious works are mostly undertaken "for the benefit of society and the bettering of mankind; the good intention of the author, therefore, should atone for his faults." Novels and works of humour are, usually, "written under every disadvantage of poverty, disease, and domestic calamity." These, and a variety of similar apologies, are to be met with in the prefatory addresses of most modern writers. And if an author were now to set out with assuring his readers, like Thucydides, that he intended his work to be a treasure for all future ages, he would be scouted as a vain and insolent fellow, and one totally unworthy the favour of the public.

A despair of hitting upon any novelty in this branch of writing had, at one time, made me resolve upon omitting the usual preface altogether; but as the property of this volume is not entirely my own, I did not think myself justified in trying any literary experiment in the present instance; and this consideration has induced me to conform to a custom so generally adopted, and to usher the following poems into the world with some few prefixed remarks. That these verses were all composed at that age when most persons think it as necessary to fall in love with the Muses to show their wit, as they do to commence their suitorship to the earthly fair ones to prove their manhood, will be discovered at a slight inspection. I am, however, not willing that they should stand absolved on this ground, being aware, that although youth may very well be considered as a fair plea for the writing, it can by no means be brought forward to excuse the publishing of bad poetry. To defend this publication, I will only confess, that I humbly apprehend the sin of appearing in print to be a trespass much more venial than the world in general are willing to allow. It is certainly the intention of every writer, however he may please himself, to please his readers; an object surely very warrantable, and which he has a right to pursue by any means that are not disgraceful or wicked. If he fail of his end, it is entirely at his own peril; or at farthest the disappointment of his bookseller; the general class of readers can suffer little or nothing by his want of success; and, to say the truth, are but very seldom cheated into any considerable loss of time or money by the continued encouragement of a dull book. We hear much of writers obtruding themselves upon the public; and a critic has a kind of poetical licence to make use of this phrase, when he mentions any silly fellow who has been incautious enough to put his crudities into print; but every one must confess, that he was never forced to buy either prose or verse in his life; and that he ought not to consider the authors of those works which he may have been tempted to procure from motives of charity, whim, and curiosity, as accountable for the bad bargains made in his literary purchases.

This defence is applied to dull, not to immoral

authors, who have, without doubt, no right to hazard the dissemination of profaneness, obscenity, or malicious falsehood. Such writers, as they apply themselves to the strongest and most prevalent passions of mankind, have but too good a chance of doing at least a temporary mischief to society; and as I am aware of the disgrace justly attached to such a conduct, I should, indeed, be ashamed if there were any thing in these verses that could scandalize virtue, or do violence to the feelings of innocence and youth.

If the delicacy of any sentimental critic should be offended with an occasional use of some plain words in part of the poems, I must hint to him that this freedom, or what he might call a coarseness of phrase, not only cannot have a pernicious effect upon any mind, but is, as it appears, perfectly necessary in some kinds of poetry, and as such has been occasionally so much introduced by the best writers in all languages, as to render any defence of its propriety altogether superfluous in this place. I will just, however, venture to assert, that no man or woman was ever made worse by reading the "Dressing Room" of Dr. Swift, which is full of terms, certainly not introduced into polite conversation; but I would not say as much of that poem of Mr. Prior's, called "Cupid Hunting," where the indelicate meaning is artfully set off, and which does not contain one ill-sounding word.

I would not by this alarm the reader into a fear of meeting with any gross or disgusting images, but merely take an opportunity of praying him not to be squeamishly angry at a few broad and open terms which will occur in the course of his perusal of this volume, and which may appear not altogether to suit the refined taste of modern readers of poetry. But as I have no intention of making this preface a vehicle for my own critical opinions, I will content myself with advertising the reader, that the poems signed L. B. are by Lord Byron; that the collector of this miscellany is answerable for such as are dated from Trinity College, Cambridge; and that the authors of the remainder of the collection have affixed distinct signatures to their respective contributions.

Trin. Coll. Camb. 1809.

CONTENTS.

PAGE

ERRATA.

Page 2. line 6. *for* ardens *read* ardent, and *f.* festur *r.* fertur.
p. 3. l. 9. *f* Who ere *r.* Whoe'er.
p. 4. l. 9. After difficile, insert est.
p. 6. l. 6 *f* Libiâ *r.* Libyâ.
p 8. l. 6. After vehemens, insert an.
p. 14. l. 12. *f.* modere *r.* mordere.
p. 15. l. 14. *f.* a humbler *r.* an humbler.
p. 17. l. 3. *f.* salad *r.* sallad.
p. 18. l. 8. *f* Castronum *r.* Castrorum.
p. 20. l. 9. *f.* repertâ *r.* reperta.
p. 21. l. last but one. *f.* launce *r.* lance.
p. 22. l. 2. *f.* hastea *r.* hastâ.
p. 28. after l. 3. insert Cæditur, et totâ sonat ulmea coena Suburrâ.
 f. exiquæ *r.* exiguæ. l. 7. *f.* calicos *r.* calices. l. 10. *f.* Latin *r.* Latinè.
p. l. 6. After diffusa, insert in.
p. l. 3. *f.* lure *r.* luce.
p. l. 2. *f* Tam *r.* Jam.
p. 30. l. 5. *f.* of day *r.* to-day.
p. 40. l. 1. *f.* ritium *r.* vitium. l. 2. *f.* animi *r.* animum. l. last. *f.* fervet *r.* ferret.
p. 42. l. last but one. *f.* et *r.* haud.
p 44. l 4. *f* malè *r.* mala. l. 7. *f.* it *r.* et.
p. 46. l. 5. After ipsa, insert hæc. l. 10. *f.* vituim *r.* vitium. l. last. talis and pravis to change places.
p. 48. l. 1. *f.* Parcuis *r.* Parciùs. l. 2. *f.* paulum *r.* paulo.
p. 49. l. last but three. *f.* ere *r.* e'er.
p. 52. l. 2. After lege, insert in.
p. 54. l. last but two. *f.* mensâ *r.* mensâve. l. last. *f.* cateni *r.* catini.
p. 56. l. last. *f.* Nomina que ivenere *r.* Nominaque invenêre.
p. 62. l. 5. *f.* Alsenus *r.* Alfenus. l. 7. After sapiens, insert operis. l. last. *f.* Lascivi *r.* Lascivi.
p. 64. l. 3. *f.* lungum *r.* longum. l. 5. *f.* sectabitor *r.* sectabitur. l. last but one. *f.* niom *r.* vicem.
p. 71 l. 1. *f.* poet—Moore *r* poet Moore,
p. 79. note. *f.* playrights *r.* playwrights.
p. 91. l. 8. *f* falters *r.* faulters.
p. 115. l. last but two. *f.* nomme *r.* nom.
p. 128. l 13. *f.* rogue *r.* rogue!
p. 153. *f.* Burns' *r.* Burns's.
p. 154. l. last. *f.* Thames' *r.* Thames's.
p. 156. note, and p. 157. ll. 7 and 8 *f.* Burns' *r.* Burns's.
p. 166. l. 2. *f.* Camoen's *r* Camoens'.
p. 170. dele A RONDEAU.

There are other mistakes and omissions, as to stops and accents, too many to set down, for which it is necessary, once for all, to crave the indulgence of the courteous reader; who, if he be conversant with the language, scarcely need be warned to put less faith in the Latin excerpts, *as here given, than in his own taste, memory, sagacity, or copy of the author imitated.*

AN

IMITATION

OF THE

ELEVENTH SATIRE OF JUVENAL.

As the following Poem was written in the year 1806, it must have, besides its own peculiar faults, the disadvantages attached to all temporary and local satires; and several of the characters therein alluded to, must, ere this, have sunk into their merited oblivion. The author, however, of this imitation trusts that, although some of the persons themselves are past away, yet as the vices which they supported are still prominent, so this attempt at exposing "costly gluttony," one of the most distinguished extravagances of the age, may not be altogether without its use. The candid critics of our times have attached no small degree of reprobation to what they call trampling upon the ashes of the dead; but the imitator of this satire freely confesses, that if he had a notice of any defunct or forgotten rogue or fool, he would with as little hesitation hitch him into a couplet, as he would attempt to shew his love of wisdom and virtue by praising the good and wise of past ages. A great painter (see Sir J. Reynolds' notes to Fresnoy's Art of Painting) has recommended the study of faulty pictures to those who would wish to excel in that art, wisely conceiving it no small advancement towards the acquisition of a good taste, to obtain a quick discernment of and proper aversion for the real defects of imperfect artists. In like manner it must appear equally useful to those who would learn to live well, to place before themselves, not only some elegant model worthy of their imitation, but some hideous original from which they must resolve to depart.

JUVENALIS SATIRA XI.

AD PERSICUM.

[1] ATTICUS eximie si cœnat, lautus habetur:
[2] Si Rutilus, demens: quid enim majore cachinno
Excipitur vulgi, quam pauper Apicius? [3] Omnis
Convictus, thermæ, stationes, omne theatrum
De Rutilo. Nam dum valida, ac juvenilia membra
Sufficiunt galeæ, dumque ardens sanguine festur
Non cogente quidem, sed nec prohibente Tribuno
Scripturus leges, et regia verba lanistæ.

TO

THE RIGHT HONOURABLE

LORD **********

---

[1] WHEN you, my lord! the splendid feast prepare
For all the nobles of St. James's air,
Who but admires the liberal, just expense,
By wealth supported, and allow'd by sense?
[2] When purse-proud Powell, in a generous vein,
Will treat the bloods and drabs of Drury Lane;
The hungry guests themselves the fool deride,
And eat his pudding, and despise his pride.
[3] Who ere frequents, or Opera, Park, or Play,
Must hear how Mara drinks her crowns away.
Proceed, fair syren! you may sip as long
As crowds admire, and courts endure your song:

[4] Multos porro vides, quos sæpe elusus ad ipsum
Creditor introïtum solet expectare macelli,
Et quibus in solo vivendi causa palato est.
Egregius cœnat meliusque miserrimus horum,
[5] Et cito casurus jam perlucente ruinâ.
Interea gustus clementa per omnia quærunt,
Nunquam animo pretiis obstantibus: interius si
Attendas, magis illa juvant quæ pluris emuntur.
[6] Ergo haud difficile perituram arcessere summam
Lancibus oppositis, vel matris imagine fracta,
Et quadringentis nummis condire gulosum

Proceed and riot, you may sing and swill
If Bath and Wells admit and listen still *.
4 Watch'd at each corner, by the race unpaid
Of every artizan, of every trade,
Dennis still thinks the world's sole good a treat,
Nor eats to live, but lives alone to eat †;
Without a meal his creditors may pine,
He still must nobly drink and nobly dine:
5 And as the meteor glares more broad and bright,
Just as it bursts and melts away in night.
Thus, in the jaws of famine and a jail,
Hesse sends him still her hog, and France her quail;
Still must he seek what swells his debts the most,
Despise the value and esteem the cost.
6 The Jews are soon his friends, and soon they fly;
But Christie's arts one dinner more supply:
Coins, plate, and pictures, some tit-bit procure,
And e'en his grandsire goes to buy liqueur.

* "Bath and Wells." Two cities in the west of England; also the title of *one bishop*.

† "Nor eats to live, but lives alone to eat." A sentence from L'Avare of Moliere.

Fictile: [7] Sic veniunt ad miscellanea ludi
[8] Refert ergo quis hæc eadem paret: in Rutilo nam
Luxuria est, in Ventidio laudabile nomen
Sumit, et a censu famam trahit. [9] Illum ego jure
Despiciam, qui scit quanto sublimior Atlas
Omnibus in Libiâ sit montibus, hic tamen idem
Ignoret quantum ferratâ distet ab arcâ
Sacculus. [10] E cœlo descendit γνῶθι σεαυτὸν
Figendum et memori tractandum pectore, sive

[7] What then must he, if scap'd the Bench and Fleet,
Who cannot treat himself, whom none will treat?
Ah! whither then from fate and famine fly,
Denied his borough and his Bellamy*?
By what new art his hunger then assuage?
Or beg or follow Caulfield to the stage.
[8] Expense in some is just, in some a shame,
In Hope we praise it, but in Bur—hs blame.
[9] And you, dear Byron! if with all your taste,
And many hours of school, not idly past;
If you, who dare to taste the sacred springs,
And boast some knowledge both of men and things;
If you, who give to every dunce his due,
And measure merit with a line so true;
If you will live the bubble of the town,
How must I smile! ah! how I ought to frown!
[10] Or great or mean the purpose of thy life,
To rule a senate, or to rule a wife;

* Surely, if I pity any man in England, it is Mr. Bellamy, who is obliged to furnish steaks and claret to a congregation of customers, none of whom need, half of whom cannot, pay him for his timely cheer. V.

Conjugium quæras, vel sacri in parte Senatûs
Esse velis. [11] Nec enim loricam poscit Achillis
Thersites, in quâ se traducebat Ulysses
Ancipitem. [12] Seu tu magno discrimine causam
Protegere affectas, te consule, dic tibi quis sis:
Orator vehemens, Curtius, an Matho. [13] Buccæ
Noscenda est mensura tuæ; spectandaque rebus
In summis, minimisque; etiam cum piscis emetu

To rise a lord of peers, or lord of pelf;
O mortal, hear this counsel—" know thyself!"
This came from heaven; to this mankind must owe
More than to all thy maxims, Rochfoucault!
11 These words are weighty, these a dunce will hear,
Jones plays the fool in his peculiar sphere *;
Nor grasps with eager hand the mace and seals,
A load that Scot resigns, and Erskine feels.
12 And you, my Lord! to this advice attend,
This from a firm, but no obtrusive friend;
Lest young ambition, eager of a name,
Should blast your talents with an early fame.
Ah! leave to longer toil and time the work,
And gradual rise, a Lansdowne or a Burke.
13 Your aim once fix'd, regard the means at first,
Nor swell at all, if when you swell you burst.
Another maxim, and that well may teach
Each striving mortal, for it suits with each;

* " Jones plays the fool in his peculiar sphere." i. e. The H—se of Com—ns, a sphere which seems to have been chosen by many for the same purpose. V.

[14] Nec mullum capias, cum sit tibi gobio tantum
In loculis: [15] quis enim te, deficiente Crumenâ,
Et crescente gulâ, manet exitus? [16] ære paterno,
Ac rebus mersis in ventrem, fœnoris, atque
Argenti gravis, & pecorum, agrorumque capacem?
Talibus a dominis post cuncta novissimus exit
Annulus, et digito mendicat Pollio nudo.
[17] Non prematuri cineres, nec funus acerbum
Luxuriæ, sed morte magis metuenda senectus.
[18] Hi plerumque gradus; conducta pecunia Romæ,

[14] Which H— should learn, nor dare again afford
With poet's purse the palate of a lord:
[15] A wretched plight is his, whate'er he thinks,
Whose maw still widens as his pocket shrinks:
[16] Lost in the gulf of one unfathom'd throat,
His houses, lands, and money to a groat:
See for a dinner Pollio suppliant stand,
A noble beggar, but without his wand*.
" [17] In prime of manhood may I nobly die,
" O'erpower'd by surfeits of my fav'rite pye;
" Nor live and linger in old age, and curse
" A tasteless palate or an empty purse."
This on a full club night is Curties prayer,
Whilst waiters wonder, and the chaplains stare.
[18] If you who saw the course which B—y ran,
Would see what other rogues and spendthrifts can,
Attend.—When empty stewards aid refuse,
They run to Britton, or some brother Jews;

* "Wand." Not a harlequin's, but a chamberlain's, or any other wand of office.

Et coram dominis consumitur. [19] Inde ubi paulum
Nescio quid superest, et pallet fœnoris auctor,
Qui vertêre solum, Baias, et ad Ostia currunt.
Cedere namque foro jam non tibi deterius, quam
Esquilias a ferventi migrare Suburra.
[20] Ille dolor solus patriam fugientibus, illa
Mœstitia est, carnisse anno Circensibus uno.
[21] Sanguinis in facie non hæret gutta; morantur
Pauci ridiculum, fugientem ex urbe pudorem.

Then live and eat, till all the thousands lent
On handsome premiums of twice ten per cent;
In Chalier's wines, or Jaquier's soups decay,
Or else in * Simkin's sauces melt away.
19 At last, when frighten'd synagogues suspect,
And friends in city and at court reject,
These bankrupts bold (an honest name) repair
On Brighton Steyne to taste the country air.
There still too nice to live on boil'd and roast,
They crack live crabs and crayfish on the coast.
20 Depress'd and vex'd 'tis true: oblig'd to stay
One spring from town, from Opera, Park, and Play:
21 Nor need they blush; for shame from Britain flies
To seek the mansion of her native skies:
And Paull alone withstands corruption's flood,
Content to be ridiculous and good †.

* "Simkin;" late proprietor of the Crown and Anchor Tavern.

† "Content to be ridiculous and good." This in Mr. Paull was a virtue so much the more disinterested, as every one must have seen the effect of his attempts; though the generous few alone might have been able to discern his noble aim. V.

[22] Experiere hodie numquid pulcherrima dictu,
Persice, non præstem vitâ, nec moribus et re;
Sed laudem siliquas occultus ganeo, pultes
Coram aliis dictem puero, sed in aure placentas.
[23] Nam, cum sis conviva mihi promissus, habebis
Evandrum, venies Tirynthius, aut minor illo
Hospes, et ipse tamen contingens sanguine cœlum;
Alter aquis, alter flammis ad sidera missus.
[24] Fereula nunc audi nullis ornata macellis.
De Tiburtino veniet pinguissimus agro
Hœdulus, et toto grege mollior, inscius herbæ,
Necdum ausus virgas humilis modere salicti,
Qui plus lactis habet quam sanguinis; et montani
Asparagi, posito quos legit villica fuso.
[25] Grandia præterea, tortoque calentia fœno
Ova adsunt ipsis cum matribus, et servatæ

22 To-day, my Lord! your wond'ring eyes shall see
How well my precepts and my life agree;
Not like the priest who calls the glutton sinner,
Then swills and surfeits at his vestry dinner.
23 To-day, since friendship calls to steal an hour
From all the noisy pomp of place and power;
As St. John once or greater Oxford sought
The bowers of Twickenham and the pensive grot;
Escap'd from courts to taste the friendly bowl,
" The feast of reason and the flow of soul;"
Do you, whate'er your short retreat reprove,
A nation's anxious care or monarch's love,
Retire to ****** well assur'd to meet
As warm a welcome, tho' a humbler treat.
24 But first, before you come my feast to share,
Pray see, without a smile, my bill of fare.
Here tender veal on early pastures fed,
Or lamb within my only cottage bred;
25 Here eggs, but not from Ireland *, fresh and warm,
And bacon, both the riches of a farm;

* " But not from Ireland." Whence most of the eggs consumed in London are brought.

Parte anni, quales fuerant in vitibus uvæ:
Signinum Syriumque pyrum: de corbibus iisdem:
Æmula Picenis, et odoris mala recentis,
Nec metuenda tibi, siccatum frigore postquam
Autumnum, et crudi posuere pericula succi.
[26] Hæc olim nostri jam luxuriosa senatûs
Cœna fuit. Curius parvo quæ legerat horto

At top a flounder, or at best a jowl;
My second course a rabbit or a fowl.
The cloth remov'd, the cheese and salad gone,
A small desert, and all unbought, comes on:
Such fruit as Vaga's blooming orchards bear,
The fragrant apple, and the mellow pear;
And nuts that well become a winter feast,
And last year's grapes, preserv'd to treat a guest.
[26] Such fare as this, believe me, once could raise
An appetite in England's better days.
Thus Temple * liv'd, his splendid labours o'er,
And found that ease he long had lov'd before
In Moore Park bowers, the bowers himself had plann'd,
Not trimm'd and twisted by a Repton's hand.

* Sir William Temple, the celebrated ambassador from the English court in the days of Charles II. to the Hague—a wise statesman, an uncorrupted patriot, and a learned man. He preserved his integrity intire in times of the most extreme corruption; and had the happiness of serving the last two monarchs of the Stuart race with fidelity, at the same time that he was the friend of William the Third. As an author he has the merit of being one of the first of English prose writers, who improved the stile of composition, and introduced an ease and purity of language before almost unknown.

Ipse focis brevibus ponebat oluscula, quæ nunc
Squallidus in magna fastidit compede fossor,
[27] Sicci terga suis, rarâ pendentia crate,
Moris erat festis quondam servare diebus,
Et natalitium cognatis ponere lardum,
Accedente novâ, si quam dabat hostia, carne.
Cognatorum aliquis titulo ter Consulis, atque
Castronum imperiis, et Dictatoris honore
Functus, ad has epulas solito maturiùs ihat,
Erectum domito referens à monte ligonem.
[28] Cum tremerent autem Fabios, durumque Catonem.
Et Scauros, et Fabricios, postremò severos
Censoris mores etiam collega timeret.

His pastures wealth, his gardens cultur'd pride,
Each moderate want, each wholesome meal supplied;
A meal, O Birch! the cits would now despise,
Who only scent from far thy sav'ry pies.
27 On festive days, just thrice a year perchance,
A well-fed buck might furnish out a haunch:
A simple pomp, and surely far the best,
That pleas'd a king, for William was his guest.
William, the prop of Europe's falling state,
And England's king, when England yet was great;
Tir'd of his subjects, one true friend to find,
The monarch left his fops and lords behind.
28 In good queen Bess' and Harry's earlier time,
Prudence was just and luxury a crime;
Then want of temperance was want of sense,
And floors of straw too cleanly gave offence *.

* "And floors of straw too cleanly gave offence." It was one article in the charges against Wolsey, that he changed the straw of his apartments too frequently.

[29] Nemo inter curas, et seria duxit habendum,
Qualis in Oceanæ fluctu testudo nataret,
Clarùm Trojugenis facturum ac nobile fulcrum
[30] Sed nudo latere, et parvis frons ærea lectis
Vile coronati caput ostendebat aselli,
Ad quod lascivi ludebant ruris alumni.
Talès ergo cibi, qualis domus, atque supellex;
Tunc rudis, et Graias mirari nescius artes;
[31] Urbibus eversis, prædarum in parte repertâ,
Magnorum artificum frangebat pocula miles,
Ut phaleris gauderet equus, celataque cassis
Romuleæ simulacra feræ mansuescere jussæ

29 A king no lover of a foreign dish *
Would hardly fit a fleet in search of fish;
Nor knew the value of the western sphere,
Which since has sent such weight of turtles here,
Dragg'd from the bosom of the Atlantic main,
To glad the peer and glut the alderman.

30 Hardy and strong (such men our age requires)
And half uncover'd, like his painted sires:
His native cottage rear'd each British son,
Not yet the sickly tenant of a town.
His dwelling simple, and his fare the same,
Supplied a mighty soul; a mighty frame,
Ere Paris, p—x, and cookery and taste
Had brought our bodies and our wits to waste.

31 Was he a soldier? to reward his toil,
His aim was glory, not ignoble spoil:
The shield emboss'd, perhaps, or silver'd launce,
The pride before, the future dread of France,

* "A king, &c." Henry VII. who refused Columbus's offers when he proposed to him to equip a fleet of discovery.

Imperii fato, et geminos sub rupe Quirinos,
Ac nudam effigiem clypeo fulgentis et bastêa,
Pendentisque Dei perituro ostenderet hosti.
Argenti quod erat, solis fulgebat in armis.
Ponebant igitur Tusco farrata catino
Omnia tunc; quibus invideas, si lividulus sis.
[32] Templorum quoque majestas præsentior, et vox
Nocte ferè mediâ mediamque audita per urbem,
Littore ab Oceani Gallis venientibus, et Diis
Officium Vatis peragentibus, his monuit nos.
[33] Hanc rebus Latiis curam præstare solebat

Except the laurels of a well-fought day,
Was all the generous victor bore away;
Or else a golden gorge or plumy crest,
And all his treasure glitter'd on his breast.
Without a softer bed or dish the more,
Content with this, the soldier still was poor:
A state how blest, and better far for health
Than Clive's large honours, or than Benfield's wealth.
32 Their island then was Heaven's peculiar care,
By day, by night, the God was present there.
And when the hostile fleets of haughty Spain*
Hung o'er the shores and cover'd all the main,
The god of battles crush'd their monarch's pride,
And rang'd his waves and storms on Britain's side.
33 And yet religion was not then an art
Where priests and pageants bear the only part.

* "And when the hostile fleets of haughty Spain," &c. The "Armada"—which was much scattered by a tempest both before and after their engagement with the English. V.

Fictilis, et nullo violatus Jupiter auro.
34 Illa domi natas, nostraque ex arbore mensas
Tempora viderunt; hos lignum stabat in usus,
Annosam si fortè nucem dejecerat Eurus.
35 At nunc divitibus cœnandi nulla voluptas,
Nil Rhombus, nil dama sapit; putere videntur
Unguenta, atque rosæ, latos nisi sustinet orbes
Grande ebur, et magno sublimis pardus biatu,

Not yet, St. Paul's! thy costly fabric shone *,
But God's own temple was the heart alone.
34 Their household goods as simple as their food,
Plates, dishes, spoons, and bowls were all of wood:
If then the gay luxurious lords forsook
Their wonted willow † for too precious oak,
The graver sort cry'd shame on such a boast,
And thought all ancient British vigour lost.
35 Our wealthy peers must even eat in state,
And scorn the dainty if without the plate.
Behold their feast! no dinner but a show,
Where glass and wax-lights glitter in a row;
High in the midst on golden columns rear'd,
Where late a plain substantial dish appear'd,

* "Not yet, St. Paul's," &c. Before the time of the present magnificent structure, there was a St. Paul's, but nothing equal in point of size or beauty to our present metropolitan church. V.

† "Willow," &c. "When our houses were builded of "willow, then had we oaken men; but now that our houses are "come to be made of oak, our men are not only become willow, "but a great many altogether of straw, which is a sore alteration." Holingshed, Description of Britain, chap. xvi.

If Holingshed complained of these men of willow, what must we in our times say? V.

Dentibus ex illis, quos mittit porta Syenes,
Et Mauri celeres, et Mauro obscurior Indus,
Et quos deposuit Nabathæo bellua saltu,
Jam nimios, capitique graves: Hinc surgit orexis
Hinc stomacho bilis. [36] Nam pes argenteus illis,
Annulus in digito quod ferrens. Ergo superbum
Convivam caveo, qui me sibi comparat, et res
Despicit exiguas, adeò nulla unica nobis
Est Eboris, nec tessellæ, nec calculus ex hâc
Materiâ: quin ipsa manubria cultellorum
Ossea: non tamen his ulla unquam obsonia fiunt
Rancidula; haud ideò pejor gallina secatur.
[37] Sed nec structor crit, cui cedere debeat omnis
Pergula, discipulus Trypheri doctoris, apud quem

A field of flowers or naked figures rise
To please the taste for show, and feed the eyes;
Whilst almost hid within the deep tureene,
Some bits from France, or German crout is seen:
No wonder, surely, if the dish excite,
More than the meat, an eager appetite.
[36] Our sires preferr'd—a thing beyond belief—
A dish of pewter—for their food was beef.
Remember, then, I bid no guest to come
That hates less splendour than he finds at home;
Pursy and proud, who cannot help compare
His dish of gold with mine of Wedgwood ware.
Of plate ten ounces scarce my board adorn,
My forks of iron, and their handles horn;
And yet my fowls are just as good, I hold,
As those with silver truss'd, or serv'd in gold.
[37] I want no master of the carving school
To slice my radishes and eggs by rule;

Sumine cum magno lepus, atque aper, et pygargus,
Et Scythicæ volucres, et Phœnicopterus ingens,
Et Gœtulus oryx, hebeti lautissima ferro.
Nec frustrum capreæ subducere, nec latus Afræ
Novit avis noster tirunclus, ac rudis omni
Tempore, et exiquæ frustis imbutus ofellæ
[38] Plebeios calicos, et paucis assibus emptos
Porriget incultus puer, atque à frigore tutus;
Non Phryx, aut Lycius, non à mangone petitus
Quisquam erit, et magno. Cum posces, posee Latin
Idem habitus cunctis, tonsi erectique capilli,
Atque hodiè tantùm proptèr convivia pexi.
Pastoris duri est hic filius, ille bubulci:

By Trusler taught to cut this way or that *,
And where to find the lean and where the fat;
To choose a pheasant's wing, but pigeon's leg,
And how to boil and break a plover's egg;
In turtle's fat to mark at once the best,
Or stuff the trail within a woodcock's breast;
All these are mysteries to household train,
Without the dainties sure the arts are vain.
[38] A country lad, with clean unpowder'd hair,
Will hand your plate and stand behind your chair;
And since the youth is neither Swiss nor French,
Won from the service of a peer or wench,
And knows no other language but his own,
In English pray let all your wants be known.
Another too, my farmer's youngest boy,
His mother's darling pride, and father's joy;
From whose fond breast nor vice nor folly blot
The sweet remembrance of his homely cot;

* "By Trusler taught to cut this way or that," &c. The Rev. Dr. Trusler, the Partridge of the age, a man of universal genius and accomplishments: for this testimony of his great abilities, consult himself, passim. V.

Suspirat longo non visam tempore matrem,
Et casulam, et notos tristis desiderat hædos:
[39] Ingenui vultùs puer, ingenuique pudoris,
Quales esse decet, quos ardens purpura vestit.
Hic tibi vina dahit diffusa montibus illis
A quibus ipse venit, quorum sub vertice lusit
Namque una atque eadem vini patria, atque ministri.
[40] Forsitan expectes, ut Gaditana canoro
Incipiat prurire choro, plausuque probari
[41] Non capit has nugas humilis domus: audiat ille
Testarum crepitus cum verbis, nudum olido stans
Fornice mancipium quibus abstinet.

His happy childhood and his rustic toil,
His simple joys, and parents tender smile;
Ready, tho' rude, supplies my butler's place
39 With blushing manners and a modest grace;
A grace how great, and more becoming far
Than Abercorn's stiff march, or Morton's star:
Just skill'd enough to hand with care about
My old October, or the foaming stout:
Or his own orchard's fruit, beneath whose shade
In early youth the tender stripling play'd.
40 Perhaps you think to meet some fiddler here,
A modish songstress, or a singing peer,
Well pleas'd to squall away their shorten'd days,
One fed with pudding, and one fed with praise.
41 Not so; I'm much too proud or much too poor
To hire a Billington, or praise a Moore *;
Let him partake such joys who joins the dance
At Ca—sh' house, with Ca—sh nymphs from France:
Palace impure, where vice and F——r reign,
Whence common girls too modest much, abstain.

* Not the poet of that name.

[42] Ille fruatur
Vocibus obscænis, omnique libidinis arte,
Qui Lacedæmonium pytismate lubricat orhem.
[43] Namque ibi fortunæ veniam damus. Alea turpis,
Turpe et adulterium mediocribus: hæc eadem illi
Omnia cum faciunt, hilares nitidique vocantur
[44] Nostra dabunt alios hodie convivia ludos.
Conditor Iliados cantabitur, atque Maronis
Altisoni dubiam facientia carmina palmam.
Quid refert tales versus quâ voce legantur?
[45] Sed nunc dilatis averte negotia curis,
Et gratam requiem dona tibi, quando licebit

42 Let him such syrens and such songs amuse,
And all the wit of Morrice' * filthy Muse;
Whom power or pride, or vice or fashion, draws
To buy a mistress as he bought a vase †.
43 Absurd, indeed, if men of nought but worth
Might reach the splendid joys of wealth and birth;
Presume—some sins polite with King to share,
And rise to all the vice of Blenheim's heir.
44 Expect no songs with me, but only hope
The strains of Dryden, or his pupil Pope:
His mighty rival on the lists of fame,
Perhaps as great, perhaps a greater name.
Strains that must please, altho' from Browne they
And tho' not set to music, musical. [fall ‡,

* I have heard that Capt. Morrice is dead. I am glad of it. I hope that his songs are dead also.

† This old fellow, wisely placed at the head of the government, has, it is said, changed his chere amie, and Mrs. B——n no longer wears the family jewels.

‡ "Altho' from Browne they fall." J. H. Browne, put for any very drawling orator.

Per totam cessare diem: non fœnoris ulla
Mentio, [46] nec primâ si lure egressa reverti
Nocte solet, tacito bilem tibi contrahat uxor,
Humida suspectis referens multitia rugis,
Vexatasque comas, et vultum auremque calentem.
[47] Protinùs ante meum, quicquid dolet, exue limen.
Pone domum, et servos, et quicquid frangitur illis,
Aut perit: ingratos ante omnia pone sodales.
[48] Interea Megalesiacæ spectacula Mappæ
Idæum solemne colunt, similisque triumpho
Prædo caballorum prætor sedet: ac mihi pace
Immensæ nimiæque licet si dicere plebis,

[45] If then, my lord! my humble fare can please,
Oh! waste with me one hour away at ease;
We from the "loop-holes of retreat" will view
The world's vain pageants, and deride them too.
To-day's your own, so mind before you come
To leave the budget with your clerks at home;
[46] Secure from all the ills of married life,
Thieves, cries, caresses, servants, children, wife!
My guest once seated in his elbow chair,
[47] The door is clos'd, and shuts out every care:
All, all must wait until our evening ends,
Peers, brokers, angry foes, and thankless friends.
[48] This day, in triumph, London's mighty mayor
Rides round his kingdoms and proclaims a fair;
His people soon in one unnumber'd throng
To Drury's splendid fane will sweep along;
Drury, whate'er the other house may say,
Quite large enough for all that love a play.
What thunders there must rend the vaulted spheres
From pit and gallery when the boy appears!

Totam hodie Romam Circus capit; et fragor aurem
Percutit, eventum viridis quo colligo panni.
Quod si deficeret, moestam attonitamque videres
Hanc urbem, veluti Cannarum in pulvere victis
Consulibus. [49] Spectent juvenes, quos clamor et audax
Sponsio, quos cultæ decet assedisse puellæ.
Spectent hoc nuptæ, juxtà recubante marito,
Quod pudeat narasse aliquem presentibus ipsis.

If cruel cholic, or as cruel cough
Should keep for once the youthful Douglas off *,
Heavens! what a sea of tears and world of groans
" Would stir to mutiny the very stones!"
All would be sad, as when the city gap'd
At Wellesley's vict'ry, and the foe escaped.
49 But plays, alas! are now but gaudy games,
Trick'd out for city drabs and city dames;
And e'en our wits contrive to hit the time
When just begins the wond'rous pantomime:
When all that suits their noble tastes engage,
Whores in the box, Grimaldi on the stage:
Devils and ghosts! a start! a cry! a groan!
And then to please the court, a windy clown †.

* I am to observe, that since the writing of this, something which I hope may be more lasting than either the cough or the cholic, namely, the good sense of the public, has kept master Betty from the London stage.

† " And then to please the court," &c. A certain pantomime, which always brought crowded houses, and was honoured by his Ma—y's and the Prin—sses company more than once, introduced this ingenious attempt at practical humour. The active operator was loudly applauded, and the performance of his slight encored. V.

N.B. " *Windy*." The clown swallowed gunpowder, and underwent all the pangs and consequences of a well dissembled cholic.

Nostra bibat vernum contracta cuticula Solem
Effugiatque togam. Tam nunc in balnea salvâ
Fronte licet vadas, quamquam solida hora supersit
Ad sextam. Facere hoc non possis quinque diebus
Continuis; quia sunt talis quoque tædia vitæ
Magna. Voluptates commendat rarior usus.

Stretch'd near my cheerful fire, I hear the clock
Just chime the quarters, and expect your knock:
Then leave the house to Lawrence, and contrive
To take for once an early meal at five;
Nor tremble, lest this taste of ease of day
Should steal your soul from public cares away:
For all our joys repeated often pall,
The joys of ease as soon perhaps as all.
Tis after sickness, health looks doubly fair,
And pleasure then most pleases, when most rare.

Trin. Coll. Camb. 1806.

HORACE.

SAT. III. LIB. I.

[1] OMNIBUS hoc ritium est cantoribus, inter amicos
Ut nunquam inducant animi cantare rogati,
Injussi nunquam desistant. Sardus habebat
Ille Tigellius hoc. Cæsar qui cogere posset
Si peteret per amicitiam patris atque suam non,
Quidquam proficeret. Si collibuisset ab ovo
Usque ad mala iteraret: Io Bacche; modo summâ
Voce, modo hac, resonat quæ chordis quatuor ima.
[2] Nil æquale bomini fuit illi: sæpe velut qui
Currebat fugiens bostem; persæpe velut qui
Junonis sacra fervet: habebat sæpe ducentos,

IMITATED.

[1] Ask modish Sirens for a song,
You must intreat the whole day long;
Make no request, and out they come,
And squeak and squall you from the room.
This fault had Sardus: oft in vain
His patron ask'd him for a strain;
Yet when he pleas'd, he struck a tune,
To last from morning unto noon:
And from his top to lowest note
Tried all the compass of his throat.
[2] To say the truth, above the ground
So strange a mortal ne'er was found;
Now quick as those whom bailiffs fright,
Now slow as coronation knight:
Now with two lacquies and a chair,
And now no barber for his hair.

Sæpe decem servos: modo reges atque tetrarchas
Omnia magna loquens; modo: sit mihi mensa tripes et
Concha salis puri, et toga quæ defendere frigus
Quàmvis crassa queat. [3] Decies centena dedisses
Huic parco paucis contento; quinque diebus
Nil erat in loculis. [4] Noctes vigilabat ad ipsum.
Manè, diem totum stertebat. Nil fuit unquam
Sic impar sibi. [5] Nunc aliquis dicat mihi: Quid tu?
Nullane habes vitia? Imo alia, et fortasse minora.
[6] Mœnius absentem Novium cum carperet· Heustu,

Now all for lords and court and show,
And now a friend and box at Kew:
With food not high, but just enough,
And coat in winter warm, tho' rough.
[3] Yet should some friend, or lucky hit,
Enrich this man of sense and wit,
Not e'en a thousand pounds would pay
Our hermit's bills at quarter day.
[4] He like the fools about the town
Would turn the world quite upside down:
Leaves daylight to the city drone,
And lives throughout the night alone:
Add that his passion, wish, and aim,
Were never for one hour the same.
[5] Some friendly list'ner says—"And you—
"Have you no faults?"—Yes, sir, a few;
I am not to my failings blind,
But think them of another kind.
[6] Sir Francis loves a sly attack
On *****'s faults behind his back.

Quidam ait, ignoras te? an ut ignotum dare nobis
Verba putas? Egomet mî ignosco, Mœnius inquit,
[7]Stultus et improbus hic amor est dignusque notari.
Cum tua prætereas oculis malè lippus inunctis.
Cur in amicorum vitiis tam cernis acutum,
Quàm aut aquila, aut serpens Epidaurius? At tibi contra
Evenit, inquirunt vitia ut tua rursus it illi.
[8]Iracundior est paulò; minùs aptus acutis
Naribus horum hominum; rideri possit, eo quod
Rusticiùs tonso toga defluit, et malè laxus
In pede calceus bæret. [9]At est bonus, ut melior vir
Non alius quisquam; at tibi amicus; at ingenium ingens
Inculto latet hoc sub corpore. [10]Denique te ipsum

Says honest George, conceal you thus
Your vices from yourself and us?
Phooh! pooh! he cries, my faults are known,
But let me keep them, they're my own.
[7] A passion this, that sure must call
For laughter and reproach from all!
Blind towards himself should B——t try
To search his friends with Lynx's eye?
Tis true, his friends as curious learn
To sound and sift him in their turn:
[8] Your friend is testy, and provokes
The humours of some waggish folks;
And fops may justly laugh—for why?
His shoes are loose, his coat awry.
[9] Yet Marcus has a generous soul,
No man a better on the whole;
With wit how bright, and heart how warm,
Beneath a rude unpolish'd form:
Add, that he loves you well beside;
[10] Then shake off all your selfish pride:

Concute, num qua tibi vitiorum inseverit olim
Natura, aut etiam consuetudo mala: [11] Namque
Neglectis urenda filix innascitur agris.
[12] Illuc prævertamur, amatorem quod amicæ
Turpia decipiunt cæcum vitia, aut etiam ipsa
Delectant; veluti Balbinum Polypus Hagnæ.
Vellem in amicitiâ sic erraremus, et isti
Errori nomen virtus posuisset honestum.
[13] At pater ut nati, sic nos debemus amici,
Si quod sit vituim, non fastidire. Strabonem
Adpellat Pætum pater, et Pullum, male parvus
Si cui filius est; ut abortivus fuit olim
Sisyphus; [14] hunc Varum distortis crusibus: illum
Balbutit Scaurum, talis fultum male pravis.

And search if any vice remain
That nature mingled with your grain;
Or such as evil habit yields:
[11] Tares flourish in neglected fields.
[12] Observe how dull the lover's sight,
The fair he thinks all over right;
No faults he sees in face or limb,
Or if he sees, they're none to him;
And wise Sir Job will love till death
His amorous Chloe's stinking breath.
Thus friends might err without a vice,
Nor be too scrupulous and nice.
[13] Let us by love paternal taught,
Not force a frown on every fault;
This father has a squinting boy,
The lad's arch eyes are all his joy:
That gets a dwarf, misshap'd and thick,
And doats upon the pretty chick.
[14] For crook-legs there are softer words,
And little hump-backs are my lord's.

[15] Parcuis hic vivit ; frugi dicatur. Ineptus
Et jactantior hic paulum est, concinnus amicis
Postulat ut videatur. At est truculentior, atque
Plus æquo liber ; simplex fortis que habeatur.
Caldior est ; acres inter numeretur. [16] Opinor
Hæc res et jungit junctos et servat amicos
At nos virtutes ipsas invertimus, atque
Sincerum cupimus vas incrustare. [17] Probus quis
Nobiscum vivit multum demissus homo ; illi
Tardo ac cognomen pingui damus. Hic fugit omnes
Insidias, nullique malo latus obdit opertum
(Cum genus hoc inter vitæ versemur ; ubi acris
Invidia, atque vigent ubi crimina ;)

15 Does one adopt a niggard plan?
Let him be call'd a prudent man.
This boasts and talks, and never ends;
A lively fellow with his friends.
Is this morose and over rude?
Esteem him brave and roughly good.
Another loves a cunning hit;
Then take him for a man of wit.
16 This happy knack at wise mistakes,
Preserves all friendships as it makes:
But we, alas! with barbarous skill,
Pervert the very good to ill;
The tainted breath of slander draws
A cloud upon the clearest vase.
17 Lives there a modest man of worth?
What's he? the dullest wretch on earth!
Should ere your cautious sense refuse
T' insure a swindler with his Jews:
(A measure just, when death or dice
May mar the captain in a trice:)

[18] Pro bene sano
Ac non incanto, fictum astutumque vocamus.
[19] Simplicior quis et est (qualem me sæpe libenter
Obtulerim libi, Mæcenas,) ut forte legentem
Aut tacitum adpellat quovis sermone molestus;
Communi sensu planè caret inquimus. [20] Eheu
Quam temere in nosmet legem sancimus iniquam:
Nam vitiis nemo sine nascitur, optimus ille est
Qui minimis urgetur. Amicus dulcis, ut æquum est,
Cum mea compensat vitiis bona, pluribus hisce

18 No former kindness then will save,
And you're a worldly-minded knave;
He's quite surpris'd his friend to find
So like the rest of all mankind.

19 If e'er a simple youth appear,
Tho' with a friend too thick and near;
(As I sometimes may seem to be,
Perchance, my B—n, e'en to thee;
Disturbing with too early knock
Your daily rest, ere two o'clock:)
Him kindly we pronounce at once
A forward fellow and a dunce.

20 Against our very selves, alas!
These penal laws we rashly pass:
For if 'tis true that since the fall,
Some sin must be the lot of all,
The best good man, it must be thought,
Is only he the least in fault.
My generous friend will fairly weigh
Each vicious and each virtuous trait;

(Si modo plura mihi bona sunt) inclinet, amari
Si volet [21] hâc lege trutinâ ponetur eâdem.
[22] Qui ne tuberibus propriis offendat amicum
Postulat; ignoscat verrucis illins. Æquum est
Peccatis veniam poscentem reddere rursus.
[23] Denique, quatenus excidi penitus vitium iræ,
Cætera item nequeunt stultis hærentia; cur non
Ponderibus modulis que suis ratio utitur? ac, res
Ut quæque est, ita suppliciis delicta cœrcct?
[24] Si quis eum servum patinam qui tollere jussus
Semesos pisces, tepidumque ligurierit jus,
In cruce suffigat. Labeone insanior inter

And if the good at all prevail,
Throw in his love to sink the scale;
[21] In this same equal balance tried,
He then may all my heart divide.
[22] Kn—t thinks his legs are no disgrace,
Then let him pardon F——'s face;
'Tis only justice to restore
That favour we receiv'd before.
[23] Since perseverance can, no doubt,
Root many mighty vices out;
But often is employ'd in vain,
'Gainst lighter follies of the brain:
In her own scales let common sense
Decide the weight of each offence;
And, as the case requires it, teach
The punishment that's due to each.
[24] Your servant tastes a dish that's left,
Should you imprison him for theft?
The world, with justice, might suppose,
Some madman had escap'd Monroe's.

Sanos dicatur. Quantò hoc furiosius, atque
Majus peccatum est? [25] paulum deliquit amicus,
(Quod nisi concedas habeare insuavis acerbus)
Odisti et fugis, ut Rufonem debitor æris;
Qui nisi, cum tristes misero venere Calendæ,
Mercedem aut nummos unde unde extricat, amaras,
Porrecto jugulo historias captivus ut audit.
[26] Comminxit lectum potus; mensà catellum
Evandri manibus tritum dejecit; ob hanc rem,
Aut positum ante meâ quiâ pullum in parte cateni

Yet there are follies worse than these,
And madder too by ten degrees.
25 The friend for whom you seem'd to live,
Has err'd at last.—Why, then, fórgive?—
Forgive! exclaim the good and wise,
But you avoid him and despise;
And fly with eager haste away,
Like debtors on a quarter day.
Who know their fate, if they should meet,
Their landlord Lewis in the street:
Condemn'd to rot in *Dorset* jails,
Or hear his verse and bitter tales;
And wait for similes and tropes,
With outstretch'd necks, like rogues for ropes.
26 Should W——r once like Fuller roar,
Or wipe his boots upon your floor;
Or with a rude, untimely paw,
Seize on your fav'rite lobster claw;
Must you, my lord! your commerce end,
And for a fish forsake a friend?

Sustulit esuriens, minus hoc jucundus amicus:
Sit mihi? Quid faciam furtum si fecerit aut, si
Prodiderit commissa fide, sponsum ve negarit?
27 Quêis paria esse ferè placuit peccata, laborant
Cum ventum ad verum est: sensus moresque repugnant,
Atque ipsa utilitas, justi prope mater et æqui.
28 Cum prorepserunt primis animalia terris,
Mutum et turpe peens, glandem atque cubilia propter,
Unguibus et pugnis, dein fustibus, atque ita porro
Pugnabant armis quæ post fabricaverat usus:
Donec verba, quibus voces sensusque notarent,
Nomina que ivenere: dehinc absistere bello.

Should he commit a real crime,
And steal your similies or rhyme;
Or else pretend that he forgets
Some guineas of his lawful debts:
Your friendship's lost—but that's no more
Than trifles forfeited before.
[27] Who say that crimes are sins alike,
At common sense and manners strike:
And e'en utility depise,
Whence equity and law arise.
[28] When creatures first at nature's birth,
Dumb, and unseemly crawl'd on earth;
For acorns and for beds of leaves,
They strove with fists, and then with staves:
Next use, with iron arms supplied,
And wars were fought, and warriors died:
Then speech was found, then language rose,
And peaceful words succeeded blows.
Now towns were built, and laws were fram'd,
That punish'd villainy, or sham'd;

Oppida cœperunt munire, et ponere leges,
Ne quis fur esset, neu latro, neu quis adulter.
[29] Nam fuit ante Helenam cunnus teterrima belli
Causa: sed ignotis perierunt mortibus illi,
Quos Veneram incertam rapientes more ferarum
Viribus editior cædebat, ut in grege taurus.
[30] Jura inventa metu injusti fateare necesse est,
Tempora si fastosque velis evolvere mundi.
Nec Natura potest justo secernere iniquum,
Dividit ut bona diversis fugienda petendis.
[31] Nec vincet ratio hoc, tantumdem ut peccet idemque,
Qui teneros caules alieni fregerit hosti,
Et qui nocturnus Divum sacra legerit. Adsit

Preserving all the goods of life,
The person, property, and wife.
[29] For women oft had been the cause
Of direful war, ere Helen was:
And men had ravish'd many a dame,
And died without the meed of fame.
Daring for lust the fell dispute,
And slaughter'd by some stronger brute.
[30] Enquire of ages past the cause,
The fear of crimes invented laws:
Not simple nature taught the skill,
To draw the line 'twixt good and ill;
'Twixt certain virtues, certain sins,
Whence merit ends, and crime begins.
[31] Nor reason, sure, can say that he
Must just as great a villain be,
Who idly breaks his neighbour's bounds,
As Melville with his thousand pounds.
Let punishments in these our times,
Variously vicious, suit our crimes:

Regula peccatis quæ pœnas irroget æquas:
Nec scuticâ dignum horribili scctere flagello.
[32] Nam, ut ferulà cædas meritum majore subire
Verbera non vereor; cum dicas esse pares res
Furta latrociniis; et magnis parva mineris
Falce recisurum simili te, si tibi regnum
Permittant homines. [33] Si dives, qui sapiens est
Et sutor bonus, et solus formosus, et est rex;
[34] Cur optas quod habes?

Nor British judges from their hall,
Send ropes for every rogue, and all.
[32] Who reads our code can never fear
A statute not enough severe.
Two rogues ascend our Newgate drop,
One robb'd th' Exchequer, one a shop;
Our modern stoic, judge in chief,
Would hang us every petty thief.
And right, quoth pious Wilberforce,
The law should always take its course.
All are, or are not free from taint,
And each is sinner if not saint:
In this the whole distinction lies,
And not in great, or good, or wise.
[33] The saint is rich; is every thing
Quite fair, good cobbler, and great king.
[34] Why then ingraft your minds a wish on,
Or try to better your condition?
If grace be all, and saints have grace,
Why seek for wealth, or power, or place?

[35] Non nosti quid pater, inquit
Chrysippus dicat: sapiens crepidas sibi nunquam
Nec soleas fecit; sutor tamen est sapiens. Quî?
" [36] Ut quamvis tacet Hermogenes, cantor tamen, atque
Optimus est modulator; ut Alsenus vafer, omni
Abjecto instrumento artis, clausâque tabernâ
Tonsor erat: sapiens sic optimus omnis
Est opifex solus, sic rex. [37] Vellunt tibi barbam
Lasciri pueri, quos tu nisi fuste coerces,

Why such a crowd of preachers sent
To India house and Parliament?
Why teize by all that's dull and odd,
The house with your damn'd neutral squad?
Why then a wish?—[35] "Sir, you neglect
One certain maxim of our sect;
Altho' the saint may never choose
To mend or make a pair of shoes;
Yet he has universal skill,
And kingdoms mends, or shoes at will;
Yet all philosophers allow
That faith can work this wonder."—How?
"[36] As Naldi tho' without a part,
May know an opera by heart;
As Douglas grown a statesman still,
Remembers how to gild a pill;
A saint can fill the best of all,
A monarch's throne, or cobbler's stall."
[37] Walk not abroad, it must be fear'd
The boys will pull your worship's beard;

Urgeris turbâ circum te stante, miserque
Rumperis et latras, magnorum maxime regum.
[38] Ne lungum faciam; dum tu quadrante lavatum
Rex ibis, neque te quisquam stipator, ineptum
Prater Crispinum, sectabitor; et mihi dulces
Ignoscent, si quid peccaro stultus, amici
Iuque niem illorum patiar delecta libenter,
Privatusque magis vivam te rege beatus.

Trust not your wisdom nor your crown,
But take a stick to keep them down.
[38] In short, go, holy monarch, rub
Your knuckles on a gospel tub;
Or mount a stool upon a common,
And frighten half-a-score old women.
No monster of perfection, I
With all my faults for pardon fly
To gentle friends, for whose dear sake
I grant th' indulgence that I take;
And find with them an happier fate
Than thou, a saint, so good and great.

From the awkwardness of the imitation, it may, perhaps, be thought that no great resemblance can be found between the ancient sage and the modern saint. Indeed, the cases are not quite parallel; but certainly, the wisdom of the Stoic, and the holiness of the Methodist, are alike in this:—that it is impossible to say whence either one or the other are derived, nor to what earthly purpose they tend.

Trin. Coll. Camb.

HORACE.

EPIST. XIX. BOOK I.

[1] Prisco si credis, Mæcenas docte, Cratino,
[2] Nulla placere diu, nec vivere, carmina possunt,
Quæ scribuntur aquæ potoribus: [3] ut male sanos
Adscripsit Liber Satyris Faunisque poëtas.
[4] Vina fere dulces oluerunt mane Camœnæ.

IMITATED.

TO ********** A WATER DRINKER.

[1] If still, my friend! no charms in wine you see,
But find that water can with wit agree;
Hear then what Bentley often would advise;
Bentley * the grave, the critic, and the wise.
" [2] He that would gain a name by tuneful rhymes,
" The present charm, and live thro' future times,
" Must leave the fools to sip at Maudlin's bowl,
" And raise, by wine, the raptures of his soul;
" [3] Miscall'd the sons of Phœbus and the Nine,
" The bards must own their sole inspirer, wine.
" [4] Wine gives the poet all his sprightly hues,
" When morning draughts assist the maudlin Muse.

* The great critic, Dr. Bentley, a wonderful genius, and remarkable for his attachment to wine. Even the amiable Mr. Cumberland, whose zeal for the character of his celebrated ancestor is surely to be admired, will not be angry at this mention of his grandfather.

[5] Laudibus arguitur vini vinosus Homerus:

[6] Ennius ipse pater nunquam, nisi potus, ad arma

Prosiluit dicenda. [7] Forum putealque Libonis

Mandabo siccis, adimam cantare severis.

[8] Hoc simul edixi, non cessavere poëtæ

" [5] Lo! all the wits of Charles and Anna's days,
" The god that fires them justly has their praise.
" [6] Our Addison, before he sweeps the strings *
" To Blenheim's heroes, and the wars of kings;
" Must taste th' ambrosia that the grape distils,
" And take his dose at Button's or at Will's.
" [7] The wreaths of Bacchus should no more entwine
" The sober lawyer than the dull divine:
" No noisy Muse, no Bacchanalian din
" Should burst the grave repose of Lincoln's Inn:
" No wits for nectar to the fount resort,
" Nor woo th' inspiring god in Figtree Court."
[8] Since this mature advice, the sons of song
Follow the drunken train and reel along:
Since this advice, the rhymster of the stews
Just throws up fifty verses ere he spews;

* Many of the most elegant and important lucubrations in the Spectator were written under the influence of wine. Mr. Addison was, perhaps, of the same nature as Lamprias, the father of Plutarch, who never philosophised so clearly, nor discoursed so elegantly, as when well heated with the juice of the grape. This Plutarch mentions of his father.

Nocturno certare mero, putere diurno.
[9] Quid? [10] Si quis vultu torvo ferus, et pede nudo,
Exiguæque togæ simulet textore Catonem;
Virtutemne repræsentet moresque Catonis?
[11] Rupit Iarbitam Timagenis æmula lingua,
Dum studet urbanus, tenditque disertus haberi,
[12] Decipit exemplar vitiis imitabile: quod si
Pallerem casu, biberent exsangue cuminum.

Thus every Julia * finds some poet—Moore
And greasy ballads greet each graceless whore.
[9] But what's the wisdom and distinction nice,
That leaves the virtue, but extracts the vice?
[10] The fool uncomb'd and wash'd but once a week,
Thinks Porson's † lice can give him Porson's Greek.
If Robson ‡ be downright, and Hanger § plain,
Is this a Shippen then, or that Montaigne?
[11] The reeling senator, so pert and young,
Who sees the commons hang on Brinsley's tongue;
Full of the rosy god, will archly cry,
"Friend Sherry's always drunk, and so am I."
[12] My Bowles, no doubt, has read how Savage far'd,
And thinks that dirt and drink bespeak a bard.

* Julia is the chief lady concerned in Mr. Little's poetical amours.

† Porson, the first Greek scholar which this or any other country has ever produced.

‡ Robson, celebrated for his speeches at the Cock and Breeches and the House of Commons.

§ Hanger, Colonel, who has been sincere enough to prophesy his future destiny in the frontispiece of his Life.

[13] O imitatores, servum pecus, ut mihi sæpe
Bilem, sæpe jocum, vestri movere tumultus!
[14] Libera per vacuum posui vestigia princeps;
Non aliena meo pressi pede. [15] Qui sibi fidit,
Dux regit examen: [16] Parios ego primus iambos
Ostendi Latio, [17] numeros animosque secutus
Archilochi, non res, et agentia verba Lycamben.

[13] O servile herd of imitators! hence
With all your borrow'd art and dull pretence;
This, this the end of all your toil, at best
To raise our anger and provoke a jest.
[14] This be my praise, "Oh, Strangford*, were it thine!"
That, not content with borrow'd plumes to shine;
Too wise to copy where I can't commend;
Too proud to call each scribbling dunce my friend;
I've left the favour'd Phœbus of the town,
And ventur'd e'en at follies all my own.
[15] (A love of glory gives to manly sense
An useful pride, a modest confidence.)
[16] This single merit may, perhaps, be mine;
To dare at last a simple, honest line
[17] 'Gainst dunces arm'd, without the power to kill,
My honest rage but wants a Gifford's † skill.

* Lord Strangford has written elegant verses, not translations of Camoens, but imitations of Mr. Little.

† The author of the Baviad and Mœviad, in the opinion of the author of this imitation, the first (almost the only) poet of the day.

[18] Ac, ne me foliis ideo brevioribus ornes,
Quod timni mutare modos et carminis artem ;
[19] Temperat Archilochi musam pede mascula Sappho,
[20] Temperat Alcæus ; sed rebus et ordine dispar ;
Nec socerum quærit, quem versibus oblinat atris,
Nec sponsæ laqueum famoso carmine nectit.
[21] Hune ego, non alio dictum prius ore, Latinus
Vulgavi fidicen : [22] juvat, immemorata ferentem,

18 Bold is the task; but not without reward,
To wield the swörd of Satire's mighty bard.
Wit still has wag'd eternal war with fools: [schools.
19 First Dryden* touch'd the state, then Pope the
20 Next Young, with all his pointed censure rose,
But vice and folly only seem'd his foes:
The times, and not the men, his page supplied,
No Ralpho hunger'd, and no Hogarth died †.
21 Since prose alone, and that beyond the Tweed ‡,
To names like these, and Gifford dare succeed;
(Thro' all the clouds of nonsense beaming forth,
A bright Aurora glitt'ring in the north;)
How great the courage, and perhaps how vain,
To venture satire in our George's reign!
22 To please the judging few be all my bent,
Their blame will punish, and their praise content:

* Dryden's Satires were chiefly political. Pope's pointed against the commentators and lumber of the schools. Dr. Young's Universal Passion was only a general Satire.

† One of whom was starved by two lines of the Dunciad, the other killed by the epistle of Churchill.

‡ The imitator here alludes to a certain Review, the best written critique on all the dull productions of the day.

Ingenuis oculisque legi, manibusque teneri.
23 Scire velis mea cur ingratus opuscula lector
Landet ametque domi, premat extra limen iniquus?
24 Non ego ventosæ plebis suffragia venor
Impensis cœnarum, et tritæ munere vestis:
25 Non ego, nobilium scriptorum auditor et ultor,
Grammaticas ambire tribus et pulpita dignor:
26 Hinc illæ lacrimæ. Spissis indigna theatris

This be my first, my last, my only aim,
And this the road I follow on to fame.
23 'Tis true, a verse like this can ne'er succeed,
Not ten will praise it, if ten thousand read.
24 Mine be this fate, my case however hard,
Not rank'd with Hafiz *, and no fav'rite bard;
Still to creep on, and still indulge my lays,
Without the vulgar itch of vulgar praise:
Too proud to buy with verse my bed and board,
And wear, like Pratt, the livery of a lord.
25 Flow smoothly, Strangford; hobble on, Carlisle,
While courts applaud, a wretch † like me may smile.
26 Pity! that shame prevents me once to try,
A tragic farce, or loyal comedy ‡;

* Hafiz, put for any admired writer in the Newspapers.

† My lord Carlisle is used, when speaking of plebeians, to denominate them poor *wretches*, unfortunate *wretches*, miserable *wretches*, &c. See his eighteen penny pamphlet, in which he draws a most pathetic picture of the crowd coming out of the play-house, and tumbling one over the other down stone stair-cases, which he proposes should be made spiral to prevent this catastrophe.

‡ *Tragic farce.* Such as the "Clock has Struck," "Rugantina," &c. &c.

Loyal comedy. Such as "The Soldier's Daughter," and fifty others full of patriotic sentiments.

Scripta pudet recitare, et nugis addere pondus,
Si dixi: [27] Rides, ait; et Jovis auribus ista
Servas: [28] fidis enim manare poëtica mella
Te solum, tibi pulcher. [29] Ad hæc ego naribus uti
Formido; et, luctantis acuto ne secer ungui,
Displicet iste locus, clamo; et diludia posco.
[30] Ludus enim genuit trepidum certamen, et iram;
Ira truces inimicitias, et funebre bellum.

Pity that I, in this well-natur'd age,
To Cherry, Hooke, and Diamond, leave the stage*.
[27] But you, my friend! with all your kindness, laugh,
And think my stile too haughty just by half:
Fit for Jove's ears, the tone's so mighty high,
And Jove alone, for none on earth will buy.
" [28] Hail! by your own applause supremely blest,
A poet you, but scribblers all the rest."
[29] Why this, my friend? and what's the crime, to fear
The pit's dire hisses and the boxes sneer?
Tho' all my friends, like L—m—b's, be true and fast,
The gods may thunder, and I'm damn'd at last.
Then angry actors, critics, all abuse,
In pamphlets, papers, journals, and reviews.
[30] Then Kemble rises, with his play-house hoards,
And Grub Street echoes with the war of words.

* These are favoured playrights.

Trin. Coll. Camb. 1807.

TRANSLATIONS FROM VOLTAIRE.

A CHARACTER.

A WOMAN, with no jealous fit,
A beauty too, but not coquette;
Of judgment sound, but learning small,
Fluent, with no pretence at all;
Nor proud nor yet familiar,
And always with an equal air.
This is my fair, the likeness right,
Not flatter'd much, nor finish'd quite.

TO A ROYAL BEAUTY.

We often find, however strange it seems,
Some facts in fiction, and some truth in dreams:
Last night my slumbers rais'd me to a throne,
And you, fair princess! were my love I own.

The gods restor'd my senses with the day,
But kindly only took my crown away.

THE CHARACTER OF

LOVE.

PROJECTS to flatter and engage the fair,
Assiduous court, and more assiduous care:
Sonnets how tender, oaths how very true!
Impressive airs!—Love does not dwell with you.
But constant passion, with no certain aim,
And soft confusion that declares the flame;
Respect most timid, with the fiercest fires,
And perseverance e'en when hope expires:
This, this is love—by this the God is known,
That holds his empire in my breast alone.

IMPROMPTU TO A

LADY.

WITH such a form divine and heavenly face,
Say, why should talents give another grace?
When from her lips such tones transporting flow,
What need that beauty should enchant us too?

Trin. Coll. Camb. 1806.

FREE TRANSLATION OF SOME PART OF

THE

SECOND ELEGY OF TIBULLUS.

Oh! give me wine, to heal my wounded breast,
And close my aching eyes in pleasant rest;
Let not a sound disturb the blissful bed,
Where love itself lies tranquil as the dead:
For cruel guards my weeping girl immure,
And heavy bolts her iron gate secure.
Gate of my rival! enemy to love!
May lightning blast thee, darted from above!
No, gentle gate! thou'lt listen to my pray'r,
Turn on thy noiseless hinge, and guide me to my fair.
Then, if a lover's madness wish'd thee ill,
Heav'n on himself avenge his guilty will.
Rather, kind gate, recal my suppliant hours,
And thy bright pillars hung with living flowers.

Thou too, my Delia, boldly brave thy guards—
Venus herself the dauntless pair rewards:
She helps the boy who jealous walls explores,
She helps the girl who opes forbidden doors,
To glide in silence from the downy bed,
To mount the staircase with a noiseless tread,
Hold the warm language of the varying eye,
And kiss by tokens when the fool is by:
Pow'rs to the favour'd few by Venus giv'n,
Betray the cuckold-making aid of heav'n.
Such arts are their's who fly from sluggard ease,
Cross the dark moor, and in the tempest freeze,
Till, safely nestling in their fair one's arms,
They feel the glowing change exalt her charms.

No lawless robber in my path shall rove,
For sacred is the messenger of love:
Nor storm nor howling rain shall cloud my road,
If Delia beckon to the lov'd abode;
Draw the soft bolt, and silently advise
My sounding footsteps with her fearful eyes,

With eager finger on her lip imprest,
Impatient brow, and quickly-beating breast.
Veil, veil your lamps, whoever travel nigh,
The thefts of Venus shun the curious eye.
Nor tread too loudly, nor inquire my name,
Nor to my face advance your taper's flame.
And ye who chance to see, the sight forswear,
And vow by all the gods ye were not there.
The prating babbler shall confess with pain
That Venus issued from the savage main.
Nay, e'en thy lord the tell-tale shall distrust,
And scorn the lying rumour of thy lust.
So sang the witch, whose prophecy divine
Assur'd my hopes, and made thee wholly mine.
She draws the stars from heaven with influence strong,
And turns the course of rapid streams by song;
Cleaves the firm ground, the dead with life inspires,
Bids rattling bones start forth from burial fires,
With magic yell the gath'ring ghosts commands,
Or purifies with milk their parting bands.

Wills she—the clouds of thunder disappear!
Wills she—dark whirlwinds overcast the sphere!
Sole mistress she of dire Medea's charms,
Her pow'r alone the dogs of hell disarms.
A rhyme she fram'd, which if thou thrice rehearse,
Thy lord shall yield such homage to the verse,
That not a tale his spies relate of me,
No, nor the hot embrace his eyes may see,
Shall win his faith:—but should my rivals dare
To snatch the slightest favour from my fair,
Her jealous spouse shall ev'ry theft perceive,
Know all he suffers, all he hears believe.

Shall I too trust the sorceress' potent art,
By herb, or song, to free my captive heart?
The lustral torches blaz'd at midnight hour;
Fell the black victim to each magic pow'r;
And thus I pray'd—" Oh! cure me not of love!
" But Delia's breast with mutual fondness move;
" I would not wish for freedom from my pains,
" Oh! what were life unless I wore her chains?"

Iron were he, who when he could possess
Thy charms, preferr'd renown to happiness.
Though deck'd with spoils, the guerdon of the brave,
O'er conquer'd lands he bids his banners wave;
While captive monarchs throng his sounding car,
And bow beneath that thunderbolt of war.
I envy not the soldier's crimson pride,
Content to feed my flocks at Delia's side.
If thou art with me, Oh! how sweet my toil,
Though doom'd to turn for bread a thankless soil!
On the lone turf to rest my weary head,
If thou art with me, Oh! how soft my bed!
What joy remains, when gentle love has flown?
On downy pillows wretched and alone,
Still thro' the night the sons of fortune weep,
Nor gold, nor blushing purple brings them sleep;
Celestial music breathes a fruitless strain,
Murmur soft airs, and fountains flow in vain.

H. F.

IN AMOREM.

CARMINA poscit Amor. Si non succendor amore,
Quî mihi sollicitus ritè canatur amor?
Sin ego crudeles teneo sub corde sagittas,
Quî possim ah! gratos scribere versiculos?
Ergò aut propositam malè rem tractare necesse est,
Aut malè compositos cogar inire modos.
Sæpe ego fæmineas ausus sum temnere formas·
Demens! nec scivi quid, rudis, esset amor.
Verùm ubi te pulchrè ridentem et dulce loquentem,
Aspexique oculos, O Galatea, tuos;
Cum voeis risûsque tui modulamina sensi
Dulcia, sensi equidem non mihi sensa priùs.
Cur mea te semper vaga mens sectatur euntem,
Curque tua ante oculos saltat imago meos?
Cur semper patulas volitat Galatea per aures?
Quàm vox grata meis auribus ista sonat!

LOVE.

Love claims the song. The bard attempts in vain
To paint the passion, till he feels the pain;
But if the cruel wound transfix his heart,
The lover's anguish checks the poet's art.
Hard then my fate, oblig'd, alas! to prove,
Unskill'd, at least, in poetry or love!
Oft have I dar'd to laugh at beauty's charms,
Her painful transports, and her sweet alarms.
But when at first I saw my smiling maid,
And all the lustre of her eyes survey'd;
When first the music of my Lydia's voice
Caught my pleas'd ear, and bade my heart rejoice;
A pleasing anguish every sense possess'd,
And unknown transports ravish'd all my breast.
Why do my thoughts still follow as she flies?
Why plays her image still before my eyes?
Why is each sound that glads my ears the same,
And softly whispers Lydia's much-lov'd name?

Quid vires animi eripuit? Cur denique somnus,
    Et ratio, atque animi pax ea grata fugit?
Heu! quid agam? quâ me soler ratione? Perirem
    Si foret in gremio fas periisse tuo.
Pectore quidnam invita meo suspiria ducit?
    Hocce quid est animo, dic, age; Num sit amor?
Quid lingnam infringit? numquid caligat ocellos?
    Quid mea suspenso membra tremore quatit?
Quid pallere facit? Quid sensus eripit omnes?
    Hocce quid est animo, dic, age; Num sit amor?
Si sit amor, (nec grande precor sit crimen amare,)
    (Sique amor his rectè significetur, amo.)
Oh amor, oh nullis hominumve Deûmve magister
    Spernende, oh miseri lente tyranne sinûs,
Aut fugiens me solve; manensve, huc lenior affer
    Delicias animæ dimidiumque meæ.

Etonæ, Dec. 1801.

What power is this that cruel steals away
By night my slumbers, and my peace by day?
Ah! what is left me, how restore my rest!
Ah! might I die, but die on Lydia's breast!
What thus with frequent sighs my breast can move?
What thus invade my bosom—is it love?
Say why before my eyes this vision swims,
My tongue why falters, and why shake my limbs?
Why thus my cheeks look pale, my senses rove?
What thus invades my bosom—is it love?
If this be love (and 'tis no crime to own
The power of love), if love by this is known,
I love, 'tis true; but, ah! thou mighty lord!
By men below and gods above ador'd;
Thou gentle tyrant of the captive soul,
Or fly and free me from thy strong controul;
Or melt my charmer, that thy bard may find
Less fierce his passion, or his fair more kind.

Trin. Coll. Camb. 1806.

THE FIRST ELEGY.

ARMS were my theme, arms late inspir'd my song,
The numbers louder, and the verse more long:
But Cupid smiling, balk'd my grave design,
And stole a foot from off my second line.
Who, cruel boy, such mighty influence gave
O'er me, the Muses bard, not Cupid's slave?
What! e'er did Venus seize Minerva's arms?
Or e'er Minerva smile in Venus charms?
Could Ceres e'er in mountain forests reign,
Or buskin'd Dian till the level plain?
Can Phœbus' hands the pointed spear require,
Or Mars's tremble on th' Aonian lyre?
Alas! e'en now too great thy large domain,
Why then ambitious ask a wider reign?

What is all thine? nor Helicon alone,
Free from thy power, nor Phœbus' lyre his own?
One nervous line my vigorous fancy brought,
He claim'd the next, and weaken'd half the thought.
Where shall I find a theme for such a song,
Or youth, or maid, with tresses flowing long?
At this complaint, Love fix'd the cruel dart,
A weapon since too fatal for my heart;
Then on his knee, the bow half-circling ply'd,
"Take for your verse, O bard, this theme!" he cried.
Ah, me! how sharp his darts is now confest,
I burn, and love alone usurps my breast!
Six feet at first, then five my flames shall tell,
Ye iron wars, ye harsher strains farewell.
Come, gentle Muse! heroic now no more,
And bind my brows with myrtles from the shore.

Trin. Coll. Camb. March, 1807.

THE

MANCIPLE'S TALE,

IMITATED FROM

CHAUCER.

Η μεγάλη παίδευσις ἐν ἀνθρώποισι σιωπή.

Vet. epig.

THOSE who are conversant with the Classics will immediately discover this tale to be founded upon the seventh fable of the second book of the Metamorphoses. Coronis is the name of the false nymph, and the story is told in a few verses beginning with a description of the tell-tale bird's former state.

It must be confessed that Chaucer has made the tale rather homely, by depriving Phœbus of his rays, and converting a mistress into a wife; a change with which the Pagan deities, any more than the modern fine gentlemen, could be not much contented. But as the Manciple's tale seems to be a vehicle for the conveyance of sentiments and maxims, rather than a story intended to please by its incidents; the ancient bard might choose to show the parties concerned as mere mortals, in order to give his wisdom an air of familiarity, and to inculcate his maxims in such a manner as might be suitable to the character from whose mouth the history proceeds. Now a Manciple, in the common acceptation of the word, was a baker, or, when most respectable, only a purveyor, to furnish bread for the tables of the nobility. Some, indeed, may conceive that his language is a little too poetical, and his learning rather more extensive, than such a condition of men is apt to acquire; and this objection will appear the better founded when that language is modernized, and that learning refined. Let not, however, any one accuse Chaucer of having ill observed the necessary conformity between sentiments and manners, between manners and characters: he has paid all the attention to this conformity which poetry will permit, as his Manciple, though not vulgar, is always plain, and displays no more wisdom but what may be collected from occasional good company and the Bible; he has but a smattering of learning, and his stock of prudence is such as the Proverbs can supply. But for this defence of the father of English verse there can be no occasion; and I should rather prepare for the glossing over of my own errors, which I will not point out, but leave to the discovery and censure of the well-natured critic.

THE

MANCIPLE'S TALE.

ERE yet (as ancient bards the tale supply)
Apollo roll'd his chariot thro' the sky,
Of goodly mortal frame, and noble mind,
He shone superior e'en amongst mankind:
But chief in every warlike sport excell'd,
And all the glorious labours of the field:
First of the youthful train the dart to throw,
Or launch the bounding arrow from the bow.

Thus, whilst the heavenly hero yet was young,
And play'd the groves and flowery meads among,
Swift from his arm the shaft unerring flew,
Pierc'd thro' his knotty scales, and Typhon slew:
As all unroll'd the sleeping serpent lay,
And bask'd and glitter'd in the noon-tide ray.

This he achiev'd, and many a glorious deed—
As poets write—and you, my friends, may read.

He too was vers'd in all the tuneful skill,
Or of the trembling harp or vocal quill:
Not e'en the royal bard, whose magic lyre
Bade Thebes with all her walls to heav'n aspire,
Tho' deft with more than mortal minstrelsy,
Was half so skill'd, or half so sweet as he.
Such was the boy; nor need the Muse declare
His form how noble, or his front how fair:
Nor outward charms alone this youth possess'd,
But generous virtues in a manly breast.
Virtues that gods themselves and heroes have,
As brave as just, and merciful as brave;
True to his trust, and to his honour true,
The flower of chivalry, and beauty too.

In wanton triumph he was wont to show,
Slung round his graceful neck the deadly bow;

And scarce of fav'rite else possess'd, beside
One only crow that did his care divide:
This in a cage he foster'd many a day,
And taught to speak as others teach a jay.
In troth this bird, like other ancient crows,
Fair as Caïster's swans, or winter snows,
Could sing a plaintive tale, as well as tell,
Clear as a lark, and sweet as Philomel.

As gods have seldom lov'd a single life,
Our Phœbus too must take a loving wife.
With him the lady liv'd completely bless'd,
By day protected, and by night caress'd:
Save that a jealous fit would sometimes rise,
To damp their joys and cloud her husband's eyes.
And yet 'tis true, of all the jealous train,
Their task is hateful, and their labour vain;
The virtuous dame, p'rhaps one in twenty score,
Is self-confin'd, and needs nor bolt nor door.
The gay coquette, whom any fool can please,
Who longs to kiss with every man she sees;

Whate'er her passion, and where'er her bent,
In spite of all, will break thro' all restraint:
Bars, bolts, and barricades before her fly,
And spouse becomes a cuckold ere he die.
Then, husbands, let your wives be unconfin'd,
And clap your padlock only on the mind.

But now to finish as I first began,
Our Phœbus did whate'er a husband can:
And still by day and night 'twas all his aim
To lead a quiet life, and please his dame.
But all in vain—for powerful nature still,
That forms the passions, and directs the will,
Works to her end, in spite of thousand foes,
Swells by restraint, and by opposing grows;
Whatever mould her plastic hands supply,
Nor art nor effort e'er can change the die.
Caught by the limed twig, or treacherous hair,
Some lively songster of the grove ensnare;
With tender care, the flutt'ring prisoner guard,
With plenty feed him, and with sweets reward.

Let glittering hues his gaudy cage enfold,
The roof of cedar, and the wires of gold;
And yet the bird, with all a captive's pain,
Still longs to seek his native wilds again;
Rejects the dainties of his varied food,
Once more to taste the berries of the wood:
And quits his cage, however warm and gay,
For houseless liberty, and flies away.

The matron's favour'd tabby, fed with milk
And choicest meats, and nurs'd on couch of silk,
If but a mouse appear upon the wall,
Flies from her milk, her meat, her couch, and all:
For cats can live without a silken house,
And milk and meat are not so good as mouse.
But these are lessons for my hearers male,
For surely, sirs, the fair are never frail.
But men, perverse by nature, all delight
To please with trulls their vulgar appetite:
What tho' their wives be noble, true, and fair,
Some low-born scrub their lewd embrace must share:

For wicked flesh, by some distinction nice,
Rejects the pleasure, if without the vice.
If right we would not, but if wrong we would,
Tho' bent to virtue, fearing to be good.
Of all our sex, this stands upon record;
But will not woman kind one tale afford?

Indeed, this Phœbus, to the lady's shame,
Had some small reason to suspect his dame;
For lewdly list'ning to old Nick's advice,
Besides her lawful lord she kept a *Vice:*
A stupid, awkward, low, untutor'd wight,
And little worthy to supplant the knight.
Such is the sex, the sinful fair ones fall,
Or to the dirtiest depths, or not at all:
The bed once void, each dunce can fill the place;
His grace's coachman oft succeeds his grace.

Thus it befell: abroad as Phœbus went,
His lady to the lusty whoreson sent.

You cry me hold—I own it for confess'd,
The plainest word of all words is the best.
By Plato, sirs, and other wits 'tis shown
That from the word alone the deed is known;
If then to speak the truth be still your aim,
Pray call each action by its proper name.
I'm a plain man, and no distinction make
Between the sins, for nobler sinners sake:
A high-born rogue is still a rogue to me,
And every whore, a whore in each degree:
The wanton dame of royal ichor full,
Or Fleet-Street drab or Covent-Garden trull.
The world, indeed, a wond'rous difference see;
Her grace is call'd his lordship's chere amie.
The hapless girl for noble sins too poor,
Is scorn'd by all a beggar and a whore:
And yet, methinks, by all the same the trade is,
And maids can lie no lower than their ladies.
The mighty rogue whose sword a kingdom wins,
The vulgar villain halter'd for his sins:

If we the purpose of their souls compare,
E'en Philip's son must own upon a par.
To fair applause with just an equal claim,
Their power but different, and their will the same:
One puts the mighty traveller in fear,
One half unpeoples half the eastern sphere.
But lo, by each a diff'rent fate is found:
The world's great robber by the world is crown'd;
The petty pilferer by the laws must fall,
Because his plunder and his sins were small.
And hence their titles, hero, king, and chief,
Adorn this rogue—but that is still a thief.
But as my wisdom is not of the school,
I know not how to prove my case by rule;
And since my simple sense can scarce avail,
Defer reflections, and resume my tale.

Pleas'd with the message of the longing dame,
To Phœbus' house the lusty whoreson came.
The longing dame, to all her vows untrue,
Of love's disport partook, and largely too.

That no one saw she thought, and no one heard;
Alas! poor fool, she quite forgot the bird.
The watchful songster from his lofty cage
Beheld the transports of their am'rous rage;
Attentive view'd the progress of the fun,
Nor sung, nor chatter'd, till the work was done.
But quite resolv'd to make my lady smart,
The foolish tell-tale took his master's part:
And when he next embrac'd his faithless bride,
" Ah! cuckoo, cuckoo—cuckoo, ah!" he cried.
Be sure that Phœbus took the words amiss,
And said, " Good bird, I pray, what tune is this?
" Not these the notes thy tongue is us'd to try,
" Not this thy song and wonted melody."
But still the silly talker perseveres,
And thus salutes the godlike cuckold's ears.
" Alas! my lord! whate'er to thee belong,
" Of worth, or beauty, or the power of song:
" Thy worth, thy beauty, they cannot avail,
" Thy songs are useless, for thy wife is frail.

" Trust to thy faithful crow, I saw her down,
" Stretch'd on that bed, and prostrate to a clown.
" What will you more?" The foolish crow combines
His wicked story with undoubted signs;
Strong was the witness certain, as, in short,
He swore he saw my lady at the sport.

Some easy London husbands would have laugh'd,
But Phœbus strung his bow and fix'd his shaft;
Then to his breast the meeting horns he bent,
And to his fair one's heart the arrow sent.
Thus did the cuckold the adult'ress slay;
Thus ends my lady; but I've more to say.
Dejected at his wife's untimely fate,
The god forgives her, but forgives too late.
Now in his grief his bow and quiver breaks,
Neglects his song and e'en his lyre forsakes;
Now blames his bird, with unavailing rage,
And thus attacks th' informer in his cage.

" Traitor accurs'd! thy lies, thy scorpion tongue
" Have done this deed, and work'd this mighty wrong.
" Oh! that thy guilty head, the cause of all,
" From Pluto's regions could my wife recal:
" The fairest, truest, best of all her kind,
" In form as beauteous, as correct in mind:
" Faultless in all as far as woman can,
" And only hapless in a jealous man.
" Fool that I was, with troubled fancies curs'd,
" To do this sin, of every sin the worst;
" To doubt my love, and yet a liar trust,
" And lay a guiltless fair one in the dust.
" Be cautious all, who see what rashness doth,
" Nor judge, nor punish on a villain's oath;
" Let proof of guilt precede the fatal blow,
" Be slow to rage, nor act before ye know:
" The rash are always fools in every age,
" And hasten only to repent their rage.
" And thou, false thief, the spring of all my woe,
" Tho' once so favour'd, now detested crow;

" Thy tongue, once eloquent, shall speak no more,
" And all the music of thy notes be o'er:
" A swarthy hue o'er all thy plumes shall spread,
" And every future crow be black from tail to head.
" Henceforth proclaim the ocean's angry swell,
" Or with hoarse screams the gathering storm foretel;
" And thro' thy future life be ever dumb,
" Save when the prophet of an ill to come:
" That all may shun thee as the bird of strife,
" And hate the tongue that slew my guiltless wife."
Thus said the angry knight, and on the word,
Stript of his plumes of white the tell-tale bird;
And cloth'd the sinner in a mournful hue,
'Reft of his power of speech and music too:
Then from his cage the hapless culprit hurl'd,
And drove away to wander thro' the world.
Since then, to satisfy one injur'd knight,
A crow has ne'er been musical nor white.

Now with th' informer's fate before your eyes,
My friend, I pray learn silence, and be wise;

And if you know a dame, for love or pelf
Who plays the whore; just keep it to yourself:
For once inform him of his lady's stains,
And straight the cuckold hates you for your pains.
The wisest of mankind has said or sung,
That 'tis the wisest thing to hold your tongue.
This I can prove, altho' unus'd to quote
The ancient maxims of the sage by rote;
For I remember what my tutor told
A man in years, and e'en in wisdom old.

"Think on the crow, and on his hapless end;
"Keep well thy tongue, if thou would'st keep thy
"A wicked tongue controul'd by no restraint [friend:
"Infects the man with one o'erclouding taint.
"Indulgent heav'n, its wanton use to bound, [round;
"With lips and teeth the tongue hath compass'd
"Thus all should look before that fence they leap,
"And learn to think whene'er they strive to speak.
"The use of speech is sure a godlike thing,
"And 'tis th' abuse alone that makes the sin;

" Yet fear thy tongue as thou would'st fear the rod,
" And ne'er be loud except in praise of God:
" The wisest lesson this for all the young,
" Perhaps the hardest, to restrain the tongue.
" Attend, my son, attend this plain advice,
" And silence keep where silence will suffice.
" Oh! learn to hate and shun a hasty word,
" That severs friendships as the flesh a sword.
" Observe the maxims of the sage that say
" (The same or Solomon, or Seneca,)
" ' Think 'tis no joy to hear the foolish rail,
" Nor listen to an angry blockhead's tale.'
" The Fleming saith, and read him all who please,
" Disturb not others, if you love your ease:
" The man is safe himself who shuns attack,
" Nor fears reproach altho' he turn his back.
" Know this of foolish truths and noxious lies
" Once said, the word irrevocable flies;
" Once past the lips, the fatal ill must come,
" And no repentance calls the mischief home.

"Love not a tale because the tale be true,
"And fly from slander whether false or true.
"Where'er thou art, amongst or high, or low,
"Keep well thy tongue, and think upon the crow."

Trin. Coll. Camb. 1804.

THE

MIRACLE.

A TALE FROM BOCCACE.

Tho' wicked Protestants would show
That miracles ceas'd long ago,
And laugh at all the pious tricks
Of Pagans and of Catholics;
Deriding equally the fancies
Of Apollonius and St. Francis;
A simple tale shall set their pride
And incredulity aside.

In Genoa, where 'twas once the fashion
To guard against the gentle passion,
By hiding half their blooming maids
For ever in a convent's shades;

A pious dame, to aid the cause
Of chastity 'gainst nature's laws,
Kept one of these religious houses,
For marrying maids to heavenly spouses:
Renown'd for prayers, and fasts, and scourging,
And dedicated to the Virgin.
And here she hid from sin and men
Of bright and holy vestals—ten:
Instructing all the virgin fair
That heav'n is won alone by prayer,
By purity, and continence,
And flying all the sins of sense.
That youth should soon the world despise,
Its miseries, and guilty joys;
From all temptation early run,
Nor nobly dare, but wisely shun;
And think it safest still and right
To gain the victory by flight.
Sermons like this, tho' mighty good,
Have little power o'er youthful blood;

And often saints, in head and heart,
Are sinners in the carnal part:
The vice is great, the truth is plain,
The dame's convinc'd, and sins again.
The abbess knew her words might fail
To purify from head to tail,
And lodg'd the sisters every one,
With lock and key, in cells of stone:
And making soul and body chaste,
To keep them virtuous—kept them fast.
Just once a day she just allow'd
A little air to cool the blood,
In her own garden, somewhat small,
And well encompass'd with a wall,
But prudently took care to find
A sorry sample of mankind,
A gard'ner old, and dumb, and lame,
With nought of man except the name;
To whom she safely dar'd confide
Her garden, and her nuns beside:

In short, the walls denied escape,
The gard'ner's age all hope of rape.
And thus the abbess fear'd no sin
From world without, or devil within.
Thus stood the case, when death that waits
At palace, and at cottage gates,
Knock'd rudely now at dumbee's door,
And kill'd him scarce alive before.
The lady abbess saw the sight,
And decently interr'd the wight.
Then search'd about for one as good,
With every right defect endow'd;
Perplex'd with anxious care to find
Another gard'ner to her mind.
For one was dumb, but young and tall,
Accomplishments less fit than all;
For what gallants can do as well
As those that kiss and cannot tell?
Another ugly, and not young,
Had too much use of ears and tongue:

For well my lady abbess knew
What harm a fluent tongue can do.
How lovely wicked wit appears!
How sin can enter by the ears!
How virtue by soft words is crost!
And she that listens once is lost!

It chanc'd there dwelt within the town
A rascal, somewhat crooked grown;
Who'd seen of merry years two score,
But look'd as old as one of four.
For drink by night, and work by day,
Had worn all manly bloom away;
And sad mishaps in love and war
Deform'd his face with many a scar.
This rogue (with every thief and whore,
Massetto was his *nomme de guerre)*
When once the news was public known
That gard'ner James at last was gone;

Resolv'd attempting to supply
His office at the nunnery:
And prompted by some devil within,
To meditate the charming sin;
Hop'd soon to find the sisterhood
Were form'd of earthly flesh and blood.
Massetto saw the job was hard—
But then, he thought on the reward:
Of young and lovely virgins ten,
In ignorance and want of men.
His wanton fancy form'd the prize;
Ten pair of rolling roguish eyes!
Ten pair of lips unskill'd to kiss,
But ripe and pouting for the bliss!
Ten bosoms fit for Venus' throne,
And all reserv'd for him alone!

The rogue, tho' ugly, still was vain,
Nor doubted all his ends to gain,

If once amongst the virgin band
He took his spade and tools in hand.
Say, Frederick, for you know what's common
To all the best and worst of woman;
Say, can your skilful highness guess,
If fortune gave the rogue success?

Chaucer, to female frailties blind,
And much a friend to all the kind,
A certain strange opinion hath,
(You read it in the wife of Bath;)
" In every station, every hour,
" Woman is fondest still of power."
But Pope *, a mighty master too,
Opines their ruling passions two;
And says, that all the sex obey
The love of pleasure or of sway:

* The collector of these poems trusts that it will not appear an improper anachronism to quote the opinion of Pope in a tale taken from Boccace, as only the outlines of the story in the original Italian are here imitated and preserved. V.

That is, the sex (to say no more)
Must play the tyrant or the whore.
What moralist shall dare decide
Between the powers of lust and pride?
The men whose wanton wives elope,
Agree, no doubt, with Mr. Pope.
Whose mates are chaster much and crosser,
Will give the preference to Dan Chaucer.
Sir Harry, and such wealthy hunks,
Who deal with peeresses or punks,
When madam scolds and thunders, own
The sex are fond of power alone.
The cautious swain who wisely roves
Thro' country towns for rural loves;
Whose mouth discreetly only waters
For milliners and farmers' daughters;
And finds Maria, Bet, and Jenny,
His own for love, or else a guinea;
From much experience thinks, no doubt,
The female world are whores throughout.
Massetto then (to say the truth,
Deep read in woman from his youth)

Confess'd this latter sage opinion,
That all are under love's dominion:
And this impell'd him much to try
His fortune at the nunnery.
He thought his figure and his face
Just suited for the gard'ner's place;
And then, 'twas only to become
For half a year both deaf and dumb.
Gods! it must be a weighty matter
That makes a blockhead cease to chatter!
And rather than his purpose balk,
Resign his right to tease and talk:
A miracle in most 'tis true,
And more than good Sir Bob could do.

With beard unshav'd, and habit poor,
To look more dirty and demure;
Massetto seeks the convent gate,
And rings the abbess to the grate:
Then bowing low, with shrugs and shakes,
And well pretended age and aches;

By signs and nods declares his aim,
And shows his fitness for the same.
The abbess could no trick suspect,
And gaz'd with joy on each defect.
"Deaf, dumb, and old, and ugly too,
"Indeed! indeed! this man will do!
"For neither wickedness nor whim
"Will meddle with a wretch like him!"
The keys are brought, the gate unbarr'd,
Massetto gains the convent yard;
And thus, thought he, old Mahomet,
To all of his believing set,
But most the rogue that fighting dies,
Unlocks the gates of paradise;
And as he opes the starry doors,
Presents a brace of heavenly whores*.
The abbess with her man content,
Massetto to the garden sent,
To pass his solitary hours
In pruning trees and wat'ring flowers.

* Houris.

For seven long days he labour'd on,
And scarcely spied a single nun;
Yet hope against despair could strive,
And longing kept his flame alive;
But fortune, that can change the dies,
And loves to favour by surprise,
Conspir'd to make Massetto blest,
Like brave Timotheus when at rest:—
(Timotheus, who could cities get,
When fortune caught them in a net.)

Thus on a sultry summer's day,
Asleep our roguish gard'ner lay,
Beneath a beach with shady boughs,
To lengthen or invite repose:
Just then the godhead, who contrives
The fall of maids, and slips of wives;
The same who found the time and place
When John the coachman met her grace;
Resolv'd two wand'ring nymphs to bring,
(The fairest pearls of all the string,)

To where Massetto still repos'd,
With many natural charms expos'd.
With half a blush, and half a smile,
The nymphs survey'd the man awhile;
His tatter'd shirt, in various parts
Discover'd charms for female hearts:
A spacious chest, a brawny back,
And skin, indeed, not very black:
Besides, a thousand nameless graces
Which girls prefer to handsome faces.
Recover'd from their first surprise,
The nuns still gaz'd with eager eyes:
When thus the younger of the twain
Her friend address'd in merry strain.

"Sure some such silly thoughts as mine
"Invade that youthful breast of thine;
"A wish, that cannot be withstood,
"That springs in every woman's blood:
"When part is known, and part is guest,
"To seek acquaintance with the rest

" Inflames my curious soul, to know
" A thing concerning all below.
" What says my sister Clara now?"
" Ah! dear Floretta, mind your vow!
" Suppose 'tis known our vows we break—
" Pray, Clara, can a dumb man speak?
" Besides, not one of all the race
" Can sure be found with heart so base,
" Who dares, of honour quite devoid,
" Expose the charms he once enjoy'd."
Clara, grown wiser now and bolder,
Just taps Massetto on the shoulder,
And makes him soon to understand
The business that they had in hand.
The happy rogue, with joy o'ercome,
But still pretending deaf and dumb,
Permits the wanton girls to lead
Within an arbour's useful shade.
What there was done, let all suppose,
The maid can guess, the matron knows.

But curiosity, that dwells
With women both in courts and cells,
Inspires a nun to know the cause
That both the happy sisters draws,
By day, by night, whate'er the weather,
To take the air so oft together.
Be sure, the truth was soon disclos'd,
And dumbee's labours all expos'd.
The nun, for girls must speak or burst,
The secret told to all at first.
The vestals then assembled straight,
A council on the culprits' fate:
Some hours in high debate were pass'd,
But this opinion rul'd at last.
" One party to the crime forgive,
" And let the guilty gard'ner live;
" But punish both the sinful fair,
" By giving—every nun her share."
The twain were griev'd, but thought it wise
To yield this man a common prize;

And thus the sisters every one
Partook the treasure, nun by nun.

Before the dame the truth suspected,
She saw her garden lay neglected;
The shrubs and flowers with drooping stalks,
And weeds in all the gravel walks;
Her wonder ceas'd, when once she knew,
The jobs her gard'ner had to do.
In such a case, the laws of Rome
Pronounc'd at once the sinner's doom:
And chastity was made to thrive,
By burying all the whores alive.
More merciful than this, the dame
Resolv'd to hide the convent's shame:
But yet condemn'd each guilty daughter
To fast a month on bread and water;
Well lectur'd every wanton elf,
And took the gard'ner—to herself.

Oblig'd to toil like any Turk,
Massetto sicken'd of his work;
For madam and her nuns besides,
Were quite enough for dumbee's sides.
(The sisters when the month was past,
Were eager all to break their fast.)
Till once upon a sabbath day,
(The dame had kept him long in play)
He found his jobs increase so fast,
That out the dumbee spoke at last.
" A cock fowl of the bantam breed
" Will serve ten hens at least in need;
" But not ten men of stoutest stuff
" Can make one woman cry 'Enough!'
" How hard must be my labour then,
" Who strive alone with more than ten?"

Down on her knees my abbess fell,
And cried aloud, " A miracle!—

" A miracle! the gard'ner speaks!
" The dumb Massetto silence breaks!"
The sisters heard the joyful sound,
And quickly all assembled round.
" Children," continued she, " prepare
" To own the power of fast and prayer.
" A mighty miracle behold,
" As great as those perform'd of old;
" By Mary's hairs, or Peter's toe,
" St. Bridget or Barromeo,
" To us the heavenly mercies reach,
" And give the dumb the power of speech.

" And you, Massetto, now proclaim
" The holy Virgin's mighty name;
" And use the speech she gave, to tell
" The wond'ring world the miracle."
Thus spoke the dame: Massetto how'd,
And sung the Virgin's praise aloud:
Whilst all the nuns her grace implor'd,
Rejoic'd to see their man restor'd.

Observing Fame directing there
Two eyes from all her thousand pair,
Chanc'd in one instant to behold
The wond'rous deed, as here 'tis told;
And blew her trump, and soon made known
The miracle thro' all the town.
And thus since then the deaf and dumb
In crowds before the convent come;
In pious hopes to gain their shares
Of comfort by the vestals prayers:
And like the blest Massetto prove
The mighty power of heavenly love.

He, happy rogue a convert grown,
With tongue and every limb his own;
Resolv'd, since she had sent his pardon,
To labour in the Virgin's garden:
And not unmindful of her favour,
Perform'd the convent's jobs for ever.

Trin. Coll. Camb. 1805.

AN

IMPROMPTU TO

A LADY SPLENDIDLY DRESSED.

WHENCE all this labour, Ah! too lovely maid!
To seek the tinsel ornaments of art?
In nature's simple dignity array'd,
'Tis yours to win, 'tis yours to keep the heart.

Let other damsels search for every toy,
Than you more studious, since than you less fair;
Let them, to gild their weaker charms, employ
The pearl's pale lustre, or the diamond's glare.

But you, Louisa, trust those killing eyes,
That blooming cheek—and, Ah! those lips divine!
Then make of every heart a willing prize,
But use your conquest only over mine.

Trin. Coll. Camb. 1806.

THE

LOVING LADY'S COMPLAINT.

A PASTORAL.

As late thro' Granta's winding vales I stray'd,
Where Camus lingers thro' his classic shade;
Borne on the breeze a plaintive murmur came,
And, mix'd with sighs, I heard Alexis' name.
'Twas Amoret beneath a beech reclin'd,
Her tresses loose, and floating in the wind,
Her hapless fate, and hopeless love she sung,
And these the notes that trembled on her tongue.

" Too lovely boy! the cause of all my pains,
Pride of the nymphs, and envy of the swains;
Here in this bower and this sequester'd grove,
To bowers and groves, ah, let me tell my love!

More kind than you, the willing Zephyrs bear
Those sighs and sorrows you disdain to hear:
Here gentle Echoes whisper back my woes,
The stream attends, and murmurs as it flows;
The turtles answer from their secret shades,
And fill with mournful music all the glades.
How weep the dewy shrubs, and droop the flowers,
How fades the green from the deserted bowers;
The leafy honours die on every tree,
And all the spring appears to mourn with me.
Too cruel boy! must you alone disdain
To hear my passion, tho' you cause my pain?

"How oft, Alexis! did my eyes reveal
The love I cannot speak, but still must feel.
How oft, dear youth! my ardent eyes confest
The living flame that burns within my breast.
Alas! when first that heavenly face I view'd,
With every charm and every grace indued;
That form where youth with blooming health com- [bines,
And beauty traces all her waving lines;

I saw, I lov'd, and tried to fly too late,
One powerful glance for ever fix'd my fate.
Thy form was all too fair, my hopes too vain,
I sigh'd and look'd, and look'd and sigh'd again.
You graceful pass'd along :—entranc'd I stood,
Afraid to follow, but my eyes pursued.
They, as the lovely image slow retir'd,
Admir'd and gaz'd, and still the more admir'd.
No longer then they view'd, but seem'd to view,
Fix'd to the spot where last your steps withdrew;
As visions bright, and, Ah! as fleeting, past
The youth away, but left a love to last.

"Ye bowers and streamlets listen to my sighs,
For you may hear me tho' the youth denies:
Ah! let your rural charms invite my boy,
And he those beauties I admire enjoy!
Then, as perhaps my lov'd Alexis leads
His lonely footsteps to your flow'ry meads,
Some happy chance your Amoret may bring
To where he wantons in your cooling spring;

Or, where on rosy beds luxuriant laid,
And lull'd to slumbers by your whispering shade;
Some golden dream his glowing fancy warms,
Flushes his cheek, and heightens all his charms.
How near him then I'll gaze! and, Ah! how near
Murmur my vows and wishes in his ear!

"Oh! that for me a happy rustic grown,
My lov'd Alexis would forsake the town;
With him, the world and all its charms I'd fly,
Not fame is sweet as such obscurity.
Content with him alone my lot to join,
And all the country's simple pleasures mine.
There, where no toils fatigue, no vices lure,
And ev'ry joy, tho' humble, still is pure;
There may we live, nor seek for wealth nor power,
And love be all the care of ev'ry hour.
(Why should I blush? Ah! blame the powers above
That made thee lovely, and that made me love.)
There, too, when youth's enraptur'd dreams are past,
The sweet remembrance of our joys may last;

Nor age, that ev'ry keener sense controuls,
Forbid the sympathy of tender souls.
And there, when fate his timely dart shall send,
(Ah! let me die, kind gods! before my friend:)
There in some grot, some cool sequester'd shade,
By former pleasures dear and sacred made;
Where all around the plaintive Zephyrs sigh,
And willows wave, and rivulets murmur by;
Your much lov'd hands a simple tomb may rear,
That only tells, 'my Amoret rests here.'
There may you oft indulge the pleasing pain,
And 'weep the more because you weep in vain.'
There on some silent morn, or pensive eve,
My watchful spirit shall your soul receive:
And, whilst the swains a common grave prepare
For one contented, ever constant pair,
Bear high away where happy angels dwell,
And find the vast reward of loving well."

Thus, thro' the evening hour the mournful maid
To calm her grief and soothe her soul essay'd;

Till in the west declining Phœhus shed
His parting beams upon the mountain's head;
The varied warblings ceased in every vale,
And nightingales took up the plaintive tale;
Homeward with footsteps slow I bent my way,
And silent darkness stole upon the day.

Trin. Coll. Camb. 1808.

EPISTLE

TO A YOUNG NOBLEMAN IN LOVE.

Hail! generous youth, whom glory's sacred flame
Inspires, and animates to deeds of fame;
Who feel the noble wish before you die
To raise the finger of each passer-by:
Hail! may a future age admiring view
A Falkland, or a Clarendon in you.

But as your blood with dangerous passion boils,
Beware! and fly from Venus' silken toils:
Ah! let the head protect the weaker heart,
And Wisdom's Ægis turn on Beauty's dart.

How weak the wit, that not content to find
Unhappy man the sport of woman kind,
Decks the fair murd'ress with imprudent skill,
And points a dart 'too apt before to kill!'

Lo! all the silly sons of Phœbus' train;
How the rapt poet turns a love-sick swain;
How shines the charmer in his flow'ry scene,
Good, fair, and powerful, Goddess, Grace, and Queen!
What wonder then that weaker mortals fail,
When genius shows her stronger armour frail?
Fools sure must err if wicked wits applaud,
And Phœhus turns a pimp, the Muse a bawd.

From you, my ***, let your friend demand
Your opening virtues for this sinking land;
Whilst " M—l—as" fond of bondage still remains,
Escaped his nurse, in younger tyrant's chains,
And gaily flutters in a female ring,
As broad as twice my lady's apron-string.
Whilst high-born C—sh hopes in time to grow,
How vast th' ambitious aim! perhaps a beau:
Ah, friend! do you such paltry joys despise,
And leave the fair and fops their mutual prize,
And aim, as youth shall ripen into man,
At nobler objects than to flirt a fan.

If you must yield to ill examples too,
And smiles and simpers have their force with you,
Let no usurping queen your bosom vex,
And if you must admire, admire the sex.
'Tis true, 'tis sad to gaze at ev'ry toast,
But 'tis a folly lasts a year at most:
The wise, if such there be, will sigh for none;
The fop for many, but the fool for one;
He, as the child would pluck one only peach,
And scorn'd the rest because within his reach,
In spite of sense, in all experience spite,
Prefers but one, where all are equal quite.
For see, in what the different charmers vary,
The same my Tearsheet, as your lady Mary:
For each would try, and just with equal skill,
And each, perhaps, may have at last her will;
Each, if a mistress now, would be a wife,
And both, believe me, will be queens for life.

But if 'tis fix'd that ev'ry lord must pair,
And you and N—d must not want an heir,

Lose not your pains, and scour the country round,
To find a treasure that can ne'er be found!
No! take the first the town or court affords,
Trick'd out to stock a market for the lords;
By chance perhaps your luckier choice may fall
On one, tho' wicked, not the worst of all:
A fair that will not seek your groom's embrace,
And just too chaste to kiss before your face;
Who, if she loves the vice, avoids the stain,
And if a ***, yet not quite a *****;
One, not a prodigal with all her sins,
And fairly spending all her pounds in pins
One, tho' perhaps as any Maxwell free,
Yet scarce a copy, Claribel, of thee:
Not very ugly, and not very old,
A little pert indeed, but not a scold;
One that, in short, may help to lead a life
Not farther much from comfort than from strife;
And when she dies, and disappoints your fears,
Shall leave some joys for your declining years.

But, as your early youth some time allows,
Nor custom yet demands you for a spouse,
Some hours of freedom may remain as yet
For one who laughs alike at love and debt:
Then, why in haste? put off the evil day,
And snatch at youthful comforts whilst you may!
Pause! nor so soon the various bliss forego
That single souls, and such alone, can know:
Ah! why too early careless life resign,
Your morning slumber, and your evening wine;
Your lov'd companion, and his easy talk;
Your Muse, invok'd in every peaceful walk.
What! can no more your scenes paternal please,
Scenes sacred long to wise, unmated ease?
The prospect lengthen'd o'er the distant down,
Lakes, meadows, rising woods, and all your own?
What! shall your N—d, shall your cloister'd bowers,
The high o'er-hanging arch and trembling towers!
Shall these, profan'd with folly or with strife,
An ever fond, or ever angry wife!

Shall these no more confess a manly sway,
But changeful woman's changing whims obey?
Who may, perhaps, as varying humour calls,
Contract your cloisters and o'erthrow your walls:
Let Repton loose o'er all the ancient ground,
Change round to square, and square convert to round;
Root up the elms and yews too solemn gloom,
And fill with shrubberies gay and green their room;
Roll down the terrace to a gay parterre,
Where gravel'd walks and flowers alternate glare;
And quite transform, in ev'ry point complete,
Your gothic abbey to a country seat.

Forget the fair one, and your fate delay;
If not avert, at least defer the day
When you beneath the female yoke shall bend,
And lose your wit, your temper, and your friend.

Trin. Coll. Camb. 1808.

LINES

ON

BEING PRESENTED WITH THE NEEDLE WORK OF

TWO LADIES.

When the first pair, ere sin and dress were known,
Roam'd thro' their native Paradise alone,
Majestic man and his celestial bride,
In nature's rich array, and blooming pride;
No blush they knew, of no reproach afraid,
But all the graces of their forms display'd:
The female, form'd upon the first great plan,
Th' immortal consort of immortal man,
Knew not the toils that household cares afford,
But shar'd the happy labours of her lord:
His fair companion, whensoe'er he shed
The grateful streams around some flow'ry bed,
Or twined their bowers, or spread their secret cell
With banks of amarinth and asphodel.

Oh! had our mother never learnt to stray,
But always lov'd and kept the virtuous way,
And never known the cares thro' all her life
That vex the dear domestic drudge—a wife!
But since the tempter warp'd her weaker mind,
And one small apple damn'd all human kind,
On all the sex immortal plagues were hurl'd,
And sin and dress then first disgrac'd the world:
For then the harder toils of life begun;
Man plough'd the ground, whilst weaker woman spun:
And thus the gentle sex, thro' ev'ry age,
The soft solicitudes of dress engage;
How just the punishment, and right the aim!
That those who caus'd the sin, should hide the shame.
With diff'rent wishes form'd, and diff'rent powers,
In active this, and that in peaceful hours.
The fiercer passions mighty man controul,
The finer feelings soothe the woman's soul:
The eagle's flame is his, but hers the dove's;
And man adores, but gentle woman loves!

Thro' all the world they bear their sep'rate parts;
These form the graceful, those the noble arts.

Nor you, ye lovely pair! those arts disdain,
Nor envy man's superior powers and pain.
God never gave those bright, those tender forms,
To till the stubborn earth, or brave the storms;
But stamp'd your frames with all the signs of grace,
With each perfection or of form or face;
To grace our pleasures, and to ease our care,
And soothe our splendid toils, but not to share.

Of Greek afraid, and not too proud to shew
That all the sex have not forgot to sew,
You choose the better part, and still despise
A woman very bold, or very wise,
Who toils and talks, and frets and fumes, poor elf!
To rise to man, but sinks below herself;
Content, whate'er such Amazons perplex,
To shine the fairest, best of all your sex.

Trin. Coll. Camb. Aug. 1806.

SONG.

BEAUTY AND WINE.

Let every true man of the Muses
    No more ask a subject from one of the Nine,
But own he's a dunce who refuses
    To sing to the praises of beauty and wine.

What joys in this earth with the blisses,
    That woman, sweet woman bestows, can compare?
E'en heaven is a heaven of kisses,
    At least if old Mahomet's Houris are there.

What misery that sorrow produces,
    But Bacchus can heal with his heavenly bowl;
The grape of all medical juices,
    Is the physic best suited to gladden the soul.

I'll not give the preference to either,
    They both are so charming, and both so divine,
But toast both their merits together;
    So fill up a bumper to beauty and wine.

I. Z.

LAMENT

FOR

ROBERT BURNS.

IMITATED FROM THE GREEK OF MOSCHUS.

Oh! injur'd bard! forgive the grateful strain
That I, the humblest of the tuneful train,
With glowing heart, yet trembling hand, repay,
For many a pensive, many a sprightly lay.

Gifford's Baviad.

Burns is no more! lament with me, ye woods,
Lament with me ye fountains and ye floods;
Let every grove in browner hues be clad,
The flowers thro' all their splendid nations sad.

It will be perhaps necessary to advertise the reader, that the imitation concludes with the 116th line of the original, as the

The blushing rose a deeper blush assume,
And fair anemones resign their bloom;
Whilst hyacinthus added sorrow shows,
Still lower droops, and still more purple grows.

"Sing, Muse of Scotia, sing the mournful strain,"
Let Philomela in her shades complain;
And on the banks of Ayr the tidings tell *,
The bard is dead that lov'd thy stream so well.
In his cold grave the rustic poet lies,
And at his death the voice of Coila dies †.

remaining verses cannot bear such a paraphrase as would suit with the rest of the poem. These words, therefore,

ἐγὼ δ' ἐπὶ πένθεϊ τῶδε
Δακρυχέων τεὸν οιτον ὀδύρομαι·

are spread out into some surface, and with them is the termination made.

* The river Ayr gives the name to Burns' native county.

† Burns calls himself the voice of Coila. Xyle being a district in Ayrshire, so called, saith tradition, from Coil, or Coilus, a Pictish monarch.

"Sing, Muse of Scotia, sing the mournful strain,"
Ye swans of Alsa cross the narrow main*:
In dying notes the poet's death declare,
To Nithsdale's nymphs and all the maids of Ayr†.

"Sing, Muse of Scotia, sing the mournful strain,"
He ne'er shall touch the tuneful reed again;
Nor e'er again beneath the lonely pine
Play to his flocks, and charm the list'ning kine:
Thro' shadowy vales he wanders now alone,
And death's dark regions echo back his moan.
Mute are the hills, the meads rejoice no more,
And all the gambols of the herds are o'er.

"Sing, Muse of Scotia, sing the mournful strain"
For Burns, each bard on Albion's happy plain;

* Alsa, a high rock opposite the coast of Ayr. The resort and habitation of sea fowl of every kind.

† The valley so called through which the "winding Nith" pursues its way.

For Burns, each liberal bosom heaves a sigh,
And gen'rous satire lifts a weeping eye*.
But Coila's nymphs his fair immortal themes
With constant tears augment the swelling streams.
The silent echos in their rocky seats,
Mourn for the song thy voice no more repeats.
The trees their fruit, the shrubs resign their flowers,
And all the verdure fades from all the bowers.
Thy fleecy flock no more their nectar yields,
Thy bees for honey cease to range the fields.
What nectar flows so sweetly as he sung?
What honey like the honey of his tongue?

"Sing, Muse of Scotia, sing the mournful strain."
Not all the dolphins shells in Triton's train;
Not all the Philomelas of the grove,
Nor swallows shrilly murmuring as they rove;
Not hapless Mary when she fondly prest
The royal infant to her aching breast;

* See the Baviad.

Not with such fierce and undissembled woes,
The mountain warriors mourn'd the brave Montrose*;
Nor with such fond regret and sorrows free,
Spread with fresh flowers thy simple tomb, Dundee †;
As Scotia now thro' all her mountains mourns
The rustic poet's death, the death of Burns.

"Sing, Muse of Scotia, sing the mournful strain;"
Nor you, ye warbling tribes, from grief refrain.
For oft he made your feather'd choirs rejoice,
Caught by his music, and improv'd your voice:
Now in your shades the grateful dirge begin,
And you, ye plaintive doves, his requiem sing.

"Sing, Muse of Scotia, sing the mournful strain:"
Ah! who can hope thy tuneful pipe to gain?

* The gallant Montrose, as he is denominated; or James Graham, marquis of Montrose.

† Lord Dundee, killed at the battle of Killicranckie pass, where there is erected to him a simple stone.

Ah! who shall wear the wreath thy temples wore?
Or press those reeds thy lips have press'd before?
For still thy breath bedews the murmuring oats,
And echo tries to catch the lingering notes.
B——es! be the treasure thine, tho' needless fear
Should keep thy music from the public ear.

"Sing, Muse of Scotia, sing the mournful strain,"
What woes oppress thy own, thy faithful Jean*!
She whose bright form thy youthful breast could move,
Awake to melody, alive to love.
She who could fly from wealth and all i s charms,
For love and poverty in Burns' arms.
Perhaps e'en now on Ayr's deserted shores
The widow'd fair one still thy fate deplores:
Or grief indulges (sorrow's sweetest boon)
In Denholm's † meads, or on the banks Doon ‡.

* Miss Jean Armour, whom he married.

† Denholm, the name of Burns' farm.

‡ Doon, a lake and river in Ayrshire, which Burns frequently names.

"Sing, Muse of Scotia, sing the mournful strain,"
For every Muse must now confess her pain.
With thee, O Burns! the power of song expires,
And all the joys the tuneful art inspires;
The lover's hopes and fears, the lover's bliss,
The youth's embraces, and the virgin's kiss.
Then round thy grave let drooping Cupids mourn,
And Venus shed her sorrows o'er thy urn.
And thou, fair stream! must share the common woe,
Whose waves for ever in his numbers flow.
Eden and Tweed could weep for Thomson's song,
And sigh'd and murmur'd as they roll'd along.
Nor shall thy current, favour'd Ayr, refuse
To sigh and murmur for thy Burns' Muse.
For each of springs, and fields, and forests sings,
Each lov'd the fields, the forests, and the springs.
But Ednam's bard aspir'd to loftier strains,
Nor always sported in the flowery plains:

* Thomson, born at Ednam in Roxburghshire.

But sung the isle amidst the waters free *,
And dar'd be loud in praise of liberty †;
And shew'd the rage which love alone controuls ‡,
And all the passions stirr'd in princely souls §.
Whilst Coila's gentle poet tunes the reeds
For ever in his groves and native meads;
Nor sings of tears, and wars destructive fires,
But amorous swains, and nymphs, and gay desires:
The look, the blush, the sigh, the kiss, th' embrace,
And all the wonders of a beauty's face.

"Sing, Muse of Scotia, sing the mournful strain,"
E'en cities lov'd the poet, tho' a swain.
Less frequent sighs, the signs of sad despair,
Heav'd the white bosoms of the British fair
When Dryden, mighty Dryden, breath'd his last,
Or when the song of Thames' swan was past;

* Britannia. † Liberty. ‡ Coriolanus.
§ Sophonisba.

Than from the cottage to the palace spread;
And told the world the bard of Ayr was dead:
The soft infection thro' Edina ran,
And mourn'd alike the poet and the man.
Nor empty sighs alone attend thy hearse,
But nobler griefs from many a plaintive verse;
E'en I must pour these numbers from my heart,
Whilst grief unfeign'd supplies the place of art.
Oh! that my simple song could half repay
The tuneful lessons that thy lines convey.

"Sing, Muse of Scotia, sing the mournful strain,"
And weep for ever, tho' you weep in vain.
The verdant herbs, the flowers, the tender shoots,
The opening buds, the blossoms, and the fruits,
In every year renew their painted pride,
By winter wither'd, but by spring supplied.
But we, the wise, the great, the lords of all,
One season flourish, then for ever fall:

Nor spring's mild breeze, nor summer's genial ray,
Can burst the tomb to animate our clay.
And thou, sweet bard, tho' all the world shall weep,
Till angels wake thee, must for ever sleep.
Nor all the songs the pensive village maid
Chaunts o'er thy grave to soothe her poet's shade,
Shall break the silence of thy peaceful shrine,
No music reach thee tho' the strain were thine.

"Sing, Muse of Scotia, sing the mournful strain;"
Can sorrow enter where the Muses reign?
Alas! unhappy bard! thy timeless fate*
Would half confess it, did I dare relate

* The editor of Burns' works draws a veil over his misfortunes, which it would be an unhallowed labour to remove. Thus much, however, must be said, that the difficulties with which the poet had to struggle did not altogether arise from his own imprudence, but rather from that suspicion which the activity of a man of genius always creates in the bosom of dunces. Of the patronage which they conferred upon the poet the Scotch have not much reason to boast, nor can praise be bestowed upon their acknowledgment of his merits when dead, whom they would not support whilst living.

Thy many struggles ere thy worth was known;
The envy, and the want that weigh'd thee down;
The slow relief that came too late to save
The broken spirit from an early grave.

Oh! that the world, tho' wide and bad, should hold
One head so wicked, and one heart so cold;
Whom Burns' simple numbers fail'd to charm,
Whom Burns' artless virtues could not warm.

"Sing, Muse of Scotia, sing the mournful strain;"
Nor want, nor envy, could that virtue stain:
But they, if such there were, whom envy fir'd,
T' oppress the man, by every Muse inspir'd,
Shall all unpitied to the grave descend,
Live without love, and die without a friend.
Whilst Burns endures an ever-glorious name,
Grav'd on the column of eternal fame;

Burns died in his 38th year, at a time when his taste must have been improved, his judgment strengthened, and all his faculties matured —at a time when many others have scarcely entered upon their course.

Of all his honours, this the least reward,
That I must rev'rence and lament the bard:
And to his much-lov'd memory grateful raise
This simple altar of unpolish'd lays.

Trin. Coll. Camb. 1804.

ON

THE DEATH OF

A YOUNG LADY.

Cecidit, velut prati
Ultimi flos, prætereunte postquam
Fractus aratro est

CATULLUS.

FROM learned solitudes where science reigns
With undivided sway o'er Granta's plains;
From cloisters echoing with no vulgar noise,
But vocal only to the Muses voice;
Say, should the murmur of a sigh arise?
Should tears e'er glisten in a student's eyes?
Can study ease the soul to grief a prey,
Books soothe the mind, and charm our woes away?

Can they recal the peace for ever fled,
Or calm my sorrows for a sister dead?
Ah! no; in vain I read, in vain peruse
What Plato taught, or woo the Mantuan Muse:
At every pause my Mary's form appears,
Awakes my mem'ry, and renews my tears.

My books I quit, and seek the lonely shades
Where elms majestic rear their leafy heads;
Where Gothic domes, and halls, old Camus laves,
And shows the classic temples in his waves.
E'en there that voice which wont to charm my ear,
Borne in soft murmurs thro' the ev'ning air,
Seems sweetest music 'midst the waving trees,
Then, lost in sighs, expires upon the breeze:
In each lone walk my Mary's form appears,
Awakes my mem'ry, and renews my tears.

Now to my couch in vain for rest I fly,
No rest awaits, tho' slumbers close my eye.

Maria comes, the same in form and face,
Those eyes of jet, those dimples rich with grace;
I fondly gaze o'er all the well known charms,
And snatch my lost Maria to my arms:
My eager transports burst the happy sleep,
I wake, to find 'twas but a dream, and weep.

Oh! ye who round a parent's marble mourn
" That virtuous age has reach'd the mortal bourn;"
Vain are your tears, those griefs unjust assuage,
Age follows youth, and death succeeds to age.
When spring's gay hours, when summer joys are past,
The grave's chill winter then must come at last.
But when the budding rose of youth displays
The golden promise of a length of days,
Who but must weep to view the faded flower
Cropt ere its prime, and in its springtide hour?
Who but must weep that youth and early bloom
Should fail to save a beauty from the tomb?

Where is that kindred soul by heaven decreed *
With her alone to live, with her to bleed,
Who, if our prayers could Mary's fate prolong,
With her had pass'd the maze of life along?
Perhaps, unconscious of those tender ties,
And her who calls him early to the skies,
Perhaps e'en now his spirit flits away
To join his Mary in the realms of day:
Or far away on angel pinions borne,
In regions fairer than the poet's morn,
Thro' heav'n's bright worlds they wing their happy flight,
And wand'ring sail on floods of purest light.

Blest maid! tho' now, where seraphs sweep the string,
Where heavenly choirs to heavenly harpings sing,
Tho' hymns divine salute thy ravish'd ears,
Awake to all the music of the spheres,
Yet, ah! attend, a voice of tuneful woe
Ascends in murmurs from the world below;

* In allusion to Dr. Watts' beautiful theory of United Souls.

Like Abel's incense, now it dares to rise,
Pass thro' the clouds, and steal into the skies.
If sighs may there be heard, if tears may flow,
If angels e'er can taste a moment's woe,
My sorrows hear, and with a sigh approve
This last sad tribute of a brother's love.

Trin. Coll. Camb. 1804.

VERSES

WRITTEN IN LORD STRANGFORD'S TRANSLATION OF CAMOENS,

AND PRESENTED TO A YOUNG LADY WHO WAS GOING TO LISBON FOR HER HEALTH.

Timidâ modò voce precamur
Ut tibi det faciles utilis aura vias.

OVID.

THIS for the fair, who every danger braves,
Nor fears to trust her beauties to the waves:
This for the fair, who quits our wintry isle,
Where one continu'd summer dares not smile;
And fearless o'er the waste of waters runs,
To happier climates warm'd by milder suns.
Where, winding from his source, thro' myrtle bowers,
To Lisbon's walls th' expanding Tagus pours:

Still blest, still rich, as when in times of old,
His streams of amber flow'd o'er sands of gold.

Accept what youth to matchless beauty gives;
Here Camoën's soul in Strangford's numbers lives.
A soul how vigorous, and how skill'd to move
All other breasts, a slave alone to love!
(Love, which all powers and passions still subdues,
And reigns triumphant even o'er the Muse.)

Such is the gift, how small for worth like thine!
How poor an off'ring at so fair a shrine!
Yet such as one whose youthful passions burn
To court the Muse, perhaps without return,
The last fond follower of the Nine may give,
And you, a Muse yourself, may well receive.

Blest shall I be who humbly view the rays
Thy brightness beams, and at a distance gaze,
If this memorial from a youth can please,
And be your fit companion thro' the seas.

Estremadura's plains may then rejoice
At Camoën's numbers and a Syren's voice:
Lisbon once more admire her poet's strain,
And Tagus waft along the well known sounds again.

Blest lands! which never frozen winters know,
Where summer's softest gales eternal blow:
Blest lands! to seek whose ever smiling plains,
The fairest of our British beauties deigns;
For her your sweets display, your joys prepare,
Whose meanest grace is, that she's passing fair.
For tho' around her all perfections strive
To give more charms than e'er had Xeuxis' five,
Hers is the beaming lustre of a soul,
Willing to yield, yet able to controul;
Hers are the beauties of th' excelling mind,
The bright idea, and the taste refin'd:
The judgment that instructs, the wit that charms,
The feeling that inspires the heart it warms:
A heart where virtue's loveliest splendours shine,
Virtue that asks a happier Muse than mine.

Ah! madam, when another nation woos
Those charms of thine that we, alas! must lose;
When at your feet the youth of Lisbon lie,
Caught by the softness of an English eye;
Whatever land you bless, where'er you go,
One thought on Albion's distant isle bestow:
One thought on those whose hearts still fondly view
Your wand'ring steps, and as you fly pursue;
Pass vales and mountains, follow o'er the sea,
And quit their native breasts to dwell with thee.
Nor wander long, but when you've cull'd each grace
The region yields to bloom upon your face,
Return to bless us once again, and bring
Th' unfading roses of a southern spring;
Return with youthful health, and charms improv'd,
Content at home to live admir'd and lov'd.

Trin. Coll. Camb. 1804

IMITATION

OF THE

SIXTH ODE, SECOND BOOK OF HORACE.

TO SEPTIMIUS.

THO' we, my friend! prepare to roam
    From happy Britain's native shore,
And leave the dear delights of home
    To hear the loud Atlantic roar:

Tho' to the distant lands we fly,
    Where desolation widely reigns,
Where Tadmor's lonely ruins lie
    On Syria's wild unpeopled plains:

This is my secret wish, to close
    My days in some secure retreat,
And from the toils of life repose,
    Content with my maternal seat.

Or if my follies or my fate
    Should that my own resort deny,
Then let me rent a small estate,
    Fast by the banks of lovely Wye.

Retir'd near Clongher's secret bowers,
    Oh! may that nook for life be mine
Where honey drops from all the flowers,
    And orchard trees excel the vine!

Where lasting frosts and tempests wild
    Nor bind the earth, nor cloud the sky,
But summers long and winters mild
    The genial tepid airs supply.

Thou too, my B——n, shalt be near
    To sooth my life, my death attend;
And weep, for thou canst weep, one tear,
    To mourn the poet and the friend.

Trin. Coll. Camb. 1809.

A RONDEAU.

θελω, θελω μανηναι.

LET prudence point her thorny way,
Let knaves invent and fools obey,
Let cowards bow to reason's shrine,
I'll be mad with love and wine.

Let the pedant proud disdain
Wit and humour's sparkling vein,
His sluggish feeling never caught
By one eccentric glowing thought;
Be the wreath of fancy mine,
I'll be mad with love and wine.

Let the envious hypocrite
False and musty saws indite;
Let the idle moralist
Mirth's entrancing sway resist;

Be the course of pleasure mine,
I'll be mad with love and wine.

Love to peace ambition charms,
Wine the care-chill'd bosom warms;
And when its powers no more inspire
Vivid wit's responsive fire;
When the jovial hours are run,
And the laugh of spirit done;
And silence with his blinking eye
Mocks the parted revelry;
Her witching dreams delight shall shed,
And yielding beauty crown my bed.

L. T.

SONG.

'Tis hard when summer clothes the year
In nature's gayest dress,
The vigorous morn of life to wear
In study's dull recess.

'Tis hard with an indignant breast,
Betray'd by secret wiles,
To meet the spoiler of its rest,
And deck the brow in smiles.

But oh! 'tis harder to conceal
A lover's pregnant sigh,
And what the secret heart doth feel,
To bid the cheek deny.

L. T.

SONG.

LET the lovesick boy, who dies
If anger beam from Cloe's eyes,
Bow before the iron rod
Of the tyrant archer god;
Who feeds with dreams of poison'd bowls
The gloomy, dull, distemper'd souls
Of wretched lovers, who despair,
Because a peevish woman's fair!

Be mine the little rosy boy
Whose only chains are chains of joy;
Who dances on to Lydian measures,
Surrounded by a troop of pleasures;
Mutual wishes, soft desires,
Such as merry May inspires,
When in the twins the sun is glowing,
And a fragrant zephyr blowing;

And sometimes round his temples twine,
A fillet steep'd in mighty wine:
But ever let the snow-wing'd dove
Of sacred faith around him move;
Let honour be his constant friend,
And secrecy his steps attend.

L. T.

THE

CONFESSION.

THE settled gaze of mute despair
Had fix'd all night the lover's eye,
A scornful beauty caus'd his care,
And hopeless passion bade him die.

The fair a happier pillow press'd,
Her cheek was flush'd with haughty joy,
The pride of conquest swell'd her breast,
And triumph lighten'd in her eye.

This youth of love, this fair of stone,
Well may I guess, but dare not shew;
Oh! had I ne'er that lady known,
I ne'er had felt that lover's woe.

L. T.

THE

RIVAL.

OH! Celia, when thine eyes of light
First broke on my enraptur'd sight,
I swore the starry train of night
Grew dim before their brilliancy:

But when I found those orbs of day
Did but thy fairer soul display,
My heart became a willing prey,
And sought a joyous slavery.

The high renown that war doth give,
With all ambition's sons receive,
Are worthless to the smiles which live
In circles of such witchery.

Not all Napoleon's fortunes prove,
Nor all Potosi's wealth should move
To tempt me from the chains of love,
From thee, my soul's idolatry.

But tho' a death I'd gladly die,
To chase the tear which fills thine eye,
And bid the troop of sorrows fly
Which dim its wonted brilliancy;

I'd rather see its magic light
Obscur'd in fate's eternal night,
Than see its potent influence bright
Shine on another's rivalry.

L. T.

WOMAN.

When by invading cares oppress'd
The drooping spirits tamely fly,
And all the hopes which youth has dress'd
In fancy's brightest colours die;

When melancholy's surly power
Weighs to despair the sinking heart,
And the dull lazy-pacing hour
Seems resting never to depart;

Say, what can bid the moments roll,
Swift as the wandering comet's glance,
Can wake to hope the fainting soul,
And bid the rising spirits dance?

What, but the smile of love and joy
That woman's dimpled cheek discloses,
And sparkles in her melting eye,
And parts her lips of living roses!

What, but her voice, whose whisper gives
    In witching music hopes of bliss;
What, but the thrilling fire which lives
    In matchless woman's yielding kiss!

L. T.

TO-DAY IS OURS, TO-MORROW IS THE GODS!

Come, let the goblet foam with generous wine,
  Spread the rich banquet, and enjoy to-day;
Haply to-morrow's sun may ne'er be thine,
  May see thee mingled with thy native clay!

The young rose smiles when fostering skies invite,
  Her blushing beauties court the kissing gale,
Her purple bosom drinks the beam of light,
  Her fragrant breath pervades the scented vale:

Her hours are few, and transient is her bloom,
  Soon fade her colours, and her graces fly,
Subject to nature's universal doom,
  She blooms to droop, and only lives to die.

Say, with a needless wisdom shall the soul
    Pine at the grief that distant years may prove?
Shall funeral garlands crown the flowing bowl?
    Or wreaths of cypress deck the couch of love?

Laugh at the clouds which threaten future sorrow;
    To present pleasures grateful homage pay;
Live while the fates allow, nor let to-morrow
    With dreams of coming anguish blast to-day!

L. T.

THE

UNGRATEFUL.

WAKE the harp to love no more!
All the flattering dream is o'er;
Wake no more the swelling measure
To the notes of former pleasure;
The powers of music fail to move
Celia's frigid heart to love!

To her magic name alone
Pour'd my harp its sweetest tone,
And sounded every thrilling wire
Celia's charms and my desire.
But now disdain usurps her eye,
Scorn dispels the rising sigh,
All the flattering dream is o'er,
Wake the harp to love no more!

Now no more with fancy's dream
Glows my harp's fantastic theme,
Grief constrains its alter'd lord,
And silence sleeps on every chord;
Save, when the winds which murmur by
Round the frame neglected sigh,
And haply from the trembling string
Some wild melodious ditty fling,
Which floats in wandering strains along,
An altered, strange, and varying song.
Strains how different far were they
Which love-inspired were wont to stray
In wildest measures o'er the lyre,
When Celia deign'd her smiles impart,
And first awoke to young desire
The thrilling pulse which warms my heart!

Then rose the song of love and joy
To melting Celia's laughing eye,
Her lips which fragrant odours flung,
Where sweet persuasion ever hung;

The warm expression of her face,
Which spoke the soul's celestial grace;
When at the tale of lover's woes,
In sighs her decent bosom rose.

Such pregnant sighs Eliza's breast,
Unconscious of their source, confess'd;
When 'mid his circling chieftains bold
His tale the graceful Trojan told.

L. T.

TO

A YOUTHFUL FRIEND.

FEW years have past since thou and I
Were firmest friends at least in name,
And childhood's gay sincerity
Preserv'd our feelings long the same.

But now, like me, too well thou know'st
What trifles oft the heart recal;
And those who once have lov'd the most,
Forget they ever lov'd at all.

And such the change thy heart displays,
So frail is early friendship's reign,
A month's brief lapse, perchance a day's,
Will view thy mind estrang'd again.

If so, it never shall be mine
    To mourn the loss of such a heart;
The fault was nature's fault, not thine,
    Which made thee fickle as thou art.

As rolls the ocean's changing tide,
    So human feelings ebb and flow;
And who would in a breast confide
    Where stormy passions ever glow?

It boots not, that together bred,
    Our childish days were days of joy,
My spring of life has quickly fled;
    Thou, too, hast ceas'd to be a boy.

And when we bid adieu to youth,
    Slaves to the specious world's controul,
We sigh a long farewel to truth;
    That world corrupts the noblest soul.

Ah, joyous season! when the mind
    Dares all things boldly but to lie,
When thought ere spoke is unconfin'd,
    And sparkles in the placid eye.

Not so in man's maturer years,
    When man himself is but a tool,
When interest sways our hopes and fears,
    And all must love and hate by rule.

With fools in kindred vice the same
    We learn at length our faults to blend;
And those, and those alone, may claim
    The prostituted name of friend.

Such is the common lot of man:
    Can we then 'scape from folly free?
Can we reverse the general plan,
    Nor be what all in turn must be?

No: for myself so dark my fate
  Through every turn of life hath been;
Man and the world so much I hate,
  I care not when I quit the scene.

But thou, with spirit frail and light,
  Wilt shine awhile and pass away,
As glow-worms sparkle thro' the night,
  But dare not stand the test of day.

Alas! whenever folly calls
  Where parasites and princes meet,
(For cherish'd first in royal halls
  The welcome vices kindly greet)

E'en now, thou'rt nightly seen to add
  One insect to the flutt'ring crowd,
And still thy trifling heart is glad
  To join the vain and court the proud.

There dost thou glide from fair to fair,
  Still simpering on with eager haste,
As flies along the gay parterre
  That taint the flowers they scarcely taste.

But say, what nymph will prize the flame?
  Which seems, as marshy vapours move,
To flit along from dame to dame,
  An ignis-fatuus gleam of love.

What friend, for thee, howe'er inclined,
  Will deign to own a kindred care?
Who will debase his manly mind,
  For friendship every fool may share?

In time forbear; amidst the throng
  No more so base a thing be seen;
No more so idly pass along,
  Be something, any thing, but—mean.

L. B.

INSCRIPTION ON THE MONUMENT

OF A

FAVOURITE DOG.

WHEN some proud son of man returns to earth,
Unknown to glory, but upheld by birth,
The sculptor's art exhausts the pomp of woe,
And storied urns record who rests below;
When all is done, upon the tomb is seen,
Not what he was, but what he should have been:
But the poor dog, in life the firmest friend,
The first to welcome, foremost to defend,
Whose honest heart is still his master's own,
Who labours, fights, lives, breathes for him alone;
Unhonour'd falls, unnotic'd all his worth,
Denied in heaven the soul he held on earth:
While man, vain insect! hopes to be forgiven,
And claims himself a sole exclusive heaven.

Oh man! thou feeble tenant of an hour,
Debas'd by slavery, or corrupt by power,
Who knows thee well must quit thee with disgust,
Degraded mass of animated dust!
Thy love is lust, thy friendship all a cheat,
Thy smiles hypocrisy, thy words deceit!
By nature vile, ennobled but by name,
Each kindred brute might bid thee blush for shame.
Ye! who perchance behold this simple urn,
Pass on,—it honours none you wish to mourn;
To mark a friend's remains these stones arise,
I knew but one unchang'd,—and here he lies.

L. B.

TO

****

WELL! thou art happy; and I feel
That I should thus be happy too,
For still my heart regards thy weal,
Warmly, as it was wont to do.

Thy husband's blest—and 'twill impart
Some pangs to view his happier lot;
But let them pass—oh! how my heart
Would hate him if he lov'd thee not!

When late I saw thy favourite child,
I thought my jealous heart would break,
But when th' unconscious infant smil'd,
I kiss'd it for its mother's sake.

I kiss'd it—and represt my sighs,
Its father in its face to see;
But then it had its mother's eyes,
And they were all to love and me.

Mary adieu! I must away,
While thou art blest, I'll not repine!
But near thee I can never stay,
My heart would soon again be thine.

I deem'd that time, I deem'd that pride
Had quench'd at length my boyish flame,
Nor knew till seated by thy side,
My heart in all,—save hope,—the same.

Yet was I calm: I knew the time
My breast would thrill before thy look,
But now to tremble were a crime,
We met—and not a nerve was shook.

I saw thee gaze upon my face,
Yet meet with no confusion there;
One only feeling couldst thou trace,
The sullen calmness of despair.

Away! away! my early dream
Remembrance never must awake:
Oh! where is Lethe's fabled stream?
My foolish heart be still, or break.

L. B.

THE

FAREWELL

TO A LADY.

WHEN man expell'd from Eden's bowers,
A moment linger'd near the gate,
Each scene recall'd the vanish'd hours,
And bade him curse his future fate.

But wandering on through distant climes,
He learnt to bear his load of grief;
Just gave a sigh to other times,
And found in busier scenes relief.

Thus, lady! will it be with me,
And I must view thy charms no more;
For whilst I linger near to thee
I sigh for all I knew before.

In flight I shall be surely wise,
    Escaping from temptation's snare;
I cannot view my Paradise
    Without a wish to enter there.

L. B.

LOVE SONG.

TO *******

REMIND me not, remind me not,
Of those belov'd, those vanish'd hours,
When all my soul was given to thee;
Hours that may never be forgot
Till time unnerves our vital powers,
And thou and I shall cease to be.

Can I forget? canst thou forget?
When playing with thy golden hair
How quick thy fluttering heart did move?
Oh! by my soul, I see thee yet,
With eyes so languid, breast so fair,
And lips, though silent, breathing love.

When thus reclining on my breast
  Those eyes threw back a glance so sweet,
    As half reproach'd, yet rais'd desire,
And still we near, and nearer prest,
  And still our glowing lips would meet,
    As if in kisses to expire.

And then those pensive eyes would close,
  And bid their lids each other seek,
    Veiling the azure orbs below;
While their long lashes' darkening gloss
  Seemed stealing o'er thy brilliant cheek,
    Like raven's plumage smooth'd on snow.

I dreamt last night our love return'd,
  And sooth to say that very dream
    Was sweeter in its phantasy
Than if for other hearts I buru'd,
  For eyes that ne'er like thine could beam
    In rapture's wild reality.

Then tell me not, remind me not
  Of hours which, though for ever gone,
    Can still a pleasing dream restore,
Till thou and I shall be forgot;
  And senseless as the mouldering stone,
    Which tells that we shall be no more.

L. B.

STANZAS

TO THE SAME.

THERE was a time, I need not name,
Since it will ne'er forgotten be,
When all our feelings were the same,
As still my soul hath been to thee.

And from that hour when first thy tongue
Confess'd a love which equall'd mine,
Though many a grief my heart hath wrung,
Unknown, and thus unfelt, by thine:

None, none, hath sunk so deep as this,
To think how all that love hath flown;
Transient as every faithless kiss,
But transient in thy breast alone.

And yet my heart some solace knew,
    When late I heard thy lips declare,
In accents once imagin'd true,
    Remembrance of the days that were.

Yes! my adored, yet most unkind!
    Though thou wilt never love again,
To me 'tis doubly sweet to find
    Remembrance of that love remain.

Yes! 'tis a glorious thought to me,
    Nor longer shall my soul repine,
Whate'er thou art, or e'er shalt be,
    Thou hast been dearly, solely mine.

L. B.

TO THE SAME.

And wilt thou weep when I am low?
Sweet lady! speak those words again;
Yet if they grieve thee, say not so,
I would not give that bosom pain.

My heart is sad, my hopes are gone,
My blood runs coldly thro' my breast;
And when I perish, thou alone
Wilt sigh above my place of rest.

And yet methinks a gleam of peace
Doth thro' my cloud of anguish shine,
And for awhile my sorrows cease
To know thy heart hath felt for mine.

Oh, lady! blessed be that tear,
  It falls for one who cannot weep;
Such precious drops are doubly dear
  To those whose eyes no tear may steep.

Sweet lady! once my heart was warm,
  With every feeling soft as thine,
But beauty's self hath ceas'd to charm
  A wretch created to repine.

Yet wilt thou weep when I am low?
  Sweet lady! speak those words again;
Yet if they grieve thee, say not so,
  I would not give that bosom pain.

L. B.

SONG.

Fill the goblet again! for I never before
Felt the glow which now gladdens my heart to its core;
Let us drink! who would not? since thro' life's varied
In the goblet alone no deception is found. [round

I have tried in its turn all that life can supply;
I have bask'd in the beam of a dark rolling eye;
I have lov'd! who has not? but what heart can declare
That pleasure existed while passion was there?

In the days of my youth, when the heart's in its spring,
And dreams that affection can never take wing,
I had friends! who has not? but what tongue will avow
That friends, rosy wine! are so faithful as thou?

The breast of a mistress some boy may estrange,
Friendship shifts with the sunbeam—thou never canst
change;
Thou grow'st old, who does not? but on earth what [appears
Whose virtues, like thine, still increase with its years?

Yet if blest to the utmost that love can bestow,
Should a rival bow down to our idol below,
We are jealous! who's not?—thou hast no such alloy,
For the more that enjoy thee, the more we enjoy.

Then the season of youth, and its vanities past,
For refuge we fly to the goblet at last;
There we find, do we not, in the flow of the soul,
That truth, as of yore, is confin'd to the bowl?

When the box of Pandora was open'd on earth,
And Misery's triumph commenc'd over Mirth;
Hope was left, was she not? but the goblet we kiss,
And care not for Hope, who are certain of bliss.

Long life to the grape! for when summer is flown
The age of our nectar shall gladden our own;
We must die, who shall not? may our sins be forgivèn,
And Hebe shall never be idle in heaven.

L. B.

HYMN TO VENUS,

FROM METASTASIO'S IMITATION OF LUCRETIUS, B. I. V. I.

OH! lovely Venus! goddess bright!
Descend in all thy glories dight;
Thou mother of almighty love,
Propitious to our homage prove!
For thou alone canst joy bestow
On gods above and men below.
Warmed by the lustre of thine eye,
    The teeming earth and azure sea
Are animate with life and joy,
    And owe their fruitfulness to thee.
Thy warm voluptuous embrace
Awakes to life the human race,
And oft the sun's warm ray beneath
Their ardent vows to thee they breathe;

Th' approach of thy benignant star,
Both clouds and tempests drives afar:
At thy command the fields appear
    In nature's gayest livery drest,
Thy voice the waves obedient hear,
    And ocean calms his heaving breast:
The stars resplendent at thy law,
The dusky veil of night can draw:
And while the frolic winds of spring
Fan the rich earth with fragrant wing,
Venus! to thee the woods among,
The birds address their votive song;
As thro' their quivering nerves they feel
Thy melting transports softly steal:
The timorous doves, thro' thee alone,
A parent's fondness cease to own;
And hastening from their young away,
Leave them to ravenous birds a prey.
To thy subduing power awake,
Their offspring tigers fierce forsake.

'Tis thy creative hand that moulds,
And every hidden form unfolds;
From thee creation's blessings flow,
To thee continued being owe;
And beauty, loveliness, and grace,
Thee, goddess, thee, their source confess.
Oh! lovely Venus! goddess bright!
Descend in all thy splendour dight!
Thou mother of almighty love,
Propitious to our homage prove!
For thou alone canst joy bestow
On gods above, and men below.

E. B.

SONNET FROM METASTASIO,

ON A LADY OF THE NAME OF ROSA ASSUMING THE RELIGIOUS HABIT.

Oh! lovely Rose! whose opening leaflets gay
The early morn unfolds with balmy dews,
Whose sweetly-modest buds at blink of day
The mildest breezes paint with vermeil hues;

Who from the soil thy tender stem has torn
To those blest regions would thy beauties doom,
Where stript of every rough and cruel thorn,
The better part of thee alone would bloom.

There shouldst thou soon become a lovely flower,
And wind, and rain, and cold, and heat, defy;
Nor feel the changeful season's transient power:
But placed beneath a watchful guardian's eye,
Shouldst ever flourish there in peace divine,
And deathless bloom to deathless fragrance join.

E. B.

THE

FAREWELL, A CANZONET,

FROM LA PARTENZA OF METASTASIO.

BEHOLD the fatal instant near,
To Laura I must bid adieu!
But how support my weary life
So distant, dearest girl! from you?
Unceasing torment I must feel,
And sigh for bliss for ever past;
But who can tell if e'er my love
On me a single thought will waste?

Yet oft in search of lost repose
My restless fancy let me bend,
To those lov'd scenes where Laura strays,
And ever on her steps attend:

Companion of your daily walk,
    My fancy still shall dwell with thee,
But you, my love !—alas ! who knows
    If e'er you waste a thought on me?

Whilst I o'er some far distant shore
    In pensive anguish bend my way,
And vainly ask the silent rocks
    Where you, my own beloved, stray;
By grief opprest from morn till morn
    My faltering voice shall call on thee,
But you, my love!—alas! who knows
    If e'er you waste a thought on me?

And oft to those enchanting scenes
    Shall I by fancy guided rove,
Where once in happiness I lived,
    For then I lived with her I love.
Ah! then what images will rise!
    How painful then will memory be!
For who can tell if e'er my love
    Will waste a single thought on me?

Here, shall I say, the fountain plays
Where anger once bedimm'd her face,
'Twas there she gave her lovely hand,
The pledge of pardon and of peace:
Here oft on pleasing hope we fed,
There we indulged in silent woes;
But now—who knows if e'er my love
A single thought on me bestows?

How many now with joyous haste
Will to your new abode repair!
How many crowd around your steps,
Their faith and love to proffer there!
Who knows amid such tender vows,
And tales of woe, and melting sighs,
Who knows if e'er my Laura feels
A single thought of me arise?

Think, Laura, of the pleasing shaft
You leave within your lover's breast;
Think how your hapless Henry loved,
Though ever hopeless to be blest;

Think on this last, this sad adieu,
 Beloved! now I bid to thee;
Think—ah! who knows if e'er my love
 Will waste a single thought on me

E. B.

ADDRESS

OF A POLISH NOBLEMAN TO HIS INFANT CHILD; FROM THE ITALIAN.

SLEEP on, sleep on, beloved boy!
  Thy hapless parents' sole delight,
May'st thou more fortunate enjoy
  A destiny than theirs more bright!

That rosy hue which decks thy cheek,
  That undisturb'd, that placid rest,
Ah! how expressively they speak
  The blameless mind, the spotless breast!

Does illness e'er excite a tear?
  Thy sorrows hush, thy tears restrain;
Thy mother soon the cause shall hear,
  And on her bosom lull thy pain.

Thy country's wrongs, thy country's woe,
My darling boy, thou can'st not mourn,
Nor the distressing transports know
By which thy parents' breasts are torn.

Thy heart unconscious does not prove,
Nor can thy little bosom rend,
The pangs of unrequited love,
The horror of a treacherous friend.

The bitter loss thou dost not feel
Of friends long lov'd, but now no more;
Nor fancy can the woes reveal
That fate for thee may have in store.

Sleep on, sleep on, my darling child!
By heaven with health and vigour blest,
May peace, with all the virtues mild,
Be ever inmates of thy breast!

E. B.

FROM THE GERMAN OF GESSNER.

THE BROKEN BOWL.

AN IDYLL.

UNDER an oak's wide spreading shade
A faun o'erpowered with sleep was laid;
Rude shepherd boys the wood-god found,
And quickly to the oak they bound;
The merry crew resolv'd to gain
A song as ransom from the chain.
They pelt him, when they've bound him fast,
With acorns till he wakes at last.
First yawn'd the faun, scarce half awake,
Then stretch'd his arms and legs, and spake:
" Where am I? where's my flute? my bowl?
" Ah! there the glittering fragments roll!

“ When drunk in sleep I sank last night,
“ I broke my bowl, my soul’s delight.
“ But who has bound me fast?” aloud
He bawl’d, and heard the giggling crowd.
“ Unbind me, boys!” again he cried;
“ Bad luck your impudence betide!”
“ No—” quick rejoin’d the festive throng,
“ Fast you remain, or sing a song.”
“ What shall I sing?” ye shepherds say:
“ Upon the bowl I’ll form my lay.”
The shepherds silent on the ground,
Then circling sate the wood-god round:
While echo, woods and dales along,
Pour’d far and near the dulcet song,
“ Broken is now the finest bowl,
“ Yonder the glittering fragments roll.

“ My cave appear’d a palace quite,
Deckt with my bowl, my soul’s delight;
To every faun this bowl divine
I offer’d, fill’d with rosy wine;

Not Pan himself with all his cost
A finer bowl could ever boast.
Broken is now my fav'rite bowl,
Yonder the glittering fragments roll.

" My brother fauns upon the ground
Sate oft this brilliant bowl around ;
And on the carving each one sung,
That drinking pass'd his lips along ;
But now, oh fauns ! ye drink no more,
Drinking and singing both are o'er,
Broken is now my fav'rite bowl,
Yonder the glittering fragments roll.

" Engraven on the bowl 'twas told
How Pan with horror struck, and cold,
Astonish'd saw the wond'rous deed,
The nymph transform'd to rustling reed ;
And how his well-known flute he made
With wax and reeds unequal laid,
And doleful music mournful play'd ;

Which echo, at the new-born sound
Startling, retold the groves around.
Broken is now the finest bowl,
Yonder the glittering fragments roll.

" There Jove, for love his bosom burn'd,
Into a bull's white form had turn'd;
There to the waves his sinews plied,
Unmindful how Europa cried;
Safe riding o'er the swelling seas,
He lick'd with flattering tongue her knees;
There trembling wrung the nymph her hands,
There griev'd her maidens on the strand;
Thro' her fair hair the Zephyrs blew,
And little Loves before her flew;
While to the ocean's utmost bound,
Laugh'd the attendant dolphins round.
Broken is now the finest bowl,
Yonder the glittering fragments roll.

"There carved was Bacchus, glorious power!
Under a cool and fragrant bower;
Form'd of a vine's o'erarching shade,
Beside was Ariadne laid;
Smiling she still repuls'd the cup,
Though yet she wish'd to drink it up;
And look'd and languish'd, sighing sweet,
And seem'd for kisses to entreat:
While round his tigers sportive play'd,
Or else with ribbands gay array'd,
Eat luscious grapes from Cupid's hand,
Or bask'd them on the sunny sand.
Broken is now this bowl divine,
Far off dispers'd the fragments shine.

"Echo! the woods and groves along
Repeat again my mournful song;
Tell it the nymphs, ye sounding waves!
Tell it the fauns thro' all their caves!
Broken is now my fav'rite bowl,
Yonder the glittering fragments roll."

So sung the faun, and then unbound,
While the gay fragments on the ground
To view, the wond'ring boys remain,
Fled swiftly o'er the verdant plain.

I. H.

FROM THE GERMAN OF GESSNER.

THE MORNING SONG.

Welcome, joyful morning ray!
Welcome, firstborn son of day!
Now the shady wood-crown d height,
Blithe thy beams are spreading o'er,
From the water glancing bright,
From the dew on every flower;
And pleasure, sprightliness, and glee,
Come with thy beams in company.

Zephyrs that in flow'rbells deep
Lay the night immers'd in sleep,
Leaving now their soft repose,
Swarm around the blushing rose;
And while they pleasing flutt'rings make,
Whispering low they seem to say,
"Sweet rose-bud! sleep'st thou yet? Awake!
"Unfold thy beauteous leaves to day."

Of ev'ry shape, and shade, and hue,
Now fly the Dreams, a motley crew;
The little Loves are wand'ring o'er
The charms on Chloe's cheek that bloom;
Ye Zephyrs, haste! from ev'ry flower,
Oh! quickly cull the rich perfume!
And ere she leaves her downy bed
The liquid fragrance o'er her shed.

Breathe gently o'er her snow-white breast,
Your od'rous sweets around her throw;
Her rosy lips with kisses taste,
And as about her couch ye blow,
The maid awake; and murm'ring tell
That long before the sun arise,
I still repeat her name with sighs,
Tell her that none e'er loved so well.

I. H. B.

TO LOVE.

THE COMPLAINT.

FROM GESSNER.

Ah, love! upon the first of May
To thee I rais'd an altar gay
Within the garden's fairest bound,
With myrtles and with roses crown'd;
And there each morn's returning light,
A garland hung with dew-drops bright.
Alas! my toil was all in vain,
Fruitless my anxious care and pain;
The flow'rs from every tree are torn,
The garden's desert and forlorn,
By raging of the wintry wind;
And Phillis too is still unkind;
Unkind as on the first of May,
And all my labour's thrown away.

I. H. B.

SONNET

FROM THE ITALIAN OF FRANCESCO REDI.

In wonted majesty and court severe
Love held his solemn parliament of late,
While guards, accustom'd to awaken fear,
Around the iron gates attentive wait.

Upon a trophied throne his arrows rear'd,
Sublime in proud magnificence he rode;
Death at his side with dire Mischance appear'd,
And Sighs, and Tears, and Grief, had there abode.

I there was dragg'd, a wretched pris'ner made,
And Love no sooner fix'd on me his eyes,
Than loud, and fierce, and pitiless he cries!
Opening his pouting lips he sternly said,
"Let him the rigour of our empire prove:"
And Fate inscrib'd the stern decree of Love.

I. H. B.

STANZAS

TO ****** ON LEAVING ENGLAND.

'Tis done—and shivering in the gale
The bark unfurls her snowy sail;
And whistling o'er the bending mast
Loud sings on high the fresh'ning blast;
And I must from this land begone,
Because I cannot love but one.

But could I be what I have been,
And could I see what I have seen,
Could I repose upon the breast
Which once my warmest wishes blest,
I should not seek another zone
Because I cannot love but one.

'Tis long since I beheld that eye
Which gave me bliss or misery;
And I have striven, but in vain,
Never to think of it again;
For tho' I fly from Albion
I still can only love but one.

As some lone bird without a mate,
My weary heart is desolate;
I look around, and cannot trace
One friendly smile or welcome face;
And e'en in crowds am still alone,
Because I cannot love but one.

And I will cross the whit'ning foam,
And I will seek a foreign home,
Till I forget a false fair face,
I ne'er shall find a resting place;
My own dark thoughts I cannot shun,
But ever love, and love but one.

The poorest, veriest wretch on earth
Still finds some hospitable hearth,
Where friendship's or love's softer glow
May smile in joy or soothe in woe;
But friend or lover I have none,
Because I cannot love but one.

I go—but wheresoe'er I flee
There's not an eye will weep for me;
There's not a kind, congenial heart
Where I can claim the meanest part:
Nor thou, who hast my hopes undone,
Wilt sigh although I love but one.

To think of every early scene,
Of what we are, and what we've been,
Would whelm some softer hearts with woe,
But mine, alas! has stood the blow;
Yet still beats on as it begun,
And never truly loves but one.

And who that dear lov'd one may be
Is not for vulgar eyes to see;
And why that early love was crost,
Thou knowst the best, I feel the most;
But few that dwell beneath the sun
Have loved so long, and loved but one.

I've tried another's fetters too,
With charms perchance as fair to view;
And I would feign have lov'd as well,
But some unconquerable spell
Forbade my bleeding breast to own
A kinded care for aught but one.

'Twould soothe to take one lingering view,
And bless thee in my last adieu;
Yet wish I not those eyes to weep
For him that wanders o'er the deep;
Tho' wheresoe'er my bark may run,
I love but thee, I love but one.

L. B.

O FONS BANDUSIÆ, &c.

O FONT! with fair unruffled face,
More clear than crystal and more bright than glass;
To thee my only bowl shall pour
The sweet libation crown'd with many a flower.
To thee a sportive kid shall bleed,
Proud of the spreading honours of his head;
Who meditates the angry shock,
For some first love the fairest of the flock.
In vain! for Venus will not save—
His youthful blood shall tinge thy azure wave.
Not Phœbus, with his summer beams,
Can penetrate thy shade, and gild thy streams;
But ever from the dog-star's heat
The wearied herds require thy green retreat.

Let other bards their fountains sing,

A bard shall love and celebrate thy spring;

The secret shelter of thy wood,

And bubbling rills that fall into thy flood.

Trin. Coll. Camb. 1805.

FROM BOILEAU.

WITH what delight rhymes on the scribbling dunce,
He's ne'er perplex'd to choose, but right at once;
With rapture hails each work as soon as done,
And wonders so much wit was all his own.
The genuine bard nor labour trusts, nor skill,
But fears a something left imperfect still;
Nor quite content, would hide behind a shelf
The work that pleases all except himself.

Trin. Coll. Camb. 1805.

——— dum serta, unguenta, puellas
Poscimus, obrepit non intellecta Senectus.

Juv.

Short is the breath of life, and short
The fleeting joys that life can give;
Those fleeting joys let wisdom court
While feeling yet and passion live.

Soon freezing age with sick distaste,
The grave of bliss, the nurse of woe,
Shall steal the wreath which nature placed
On joyous youth's exulting brow.

While yet the swelling goblet flows,
And sorrow yields to revel's power,
While blossoms yet the breathing rose,
And laughter speeds the jovial hour:

While yet in ardent youth we fly,
Pregnant of life and hope, to sip
Nectareous dew, entrancing joy!
From blushing beauty's rosy lip:

Their sudden shafts the Fates dispense,
And wither all the beauteous dream,
Or tasteless age steeps every sense
In apathy's oblivious stream.

Then still while love and young desire
Play thro' the veins and warm the soul,
Burn, burn with love's exalting fire,
And drink to beauty's health the bowl.

L. T.

UNDER THE PICTURE OF

LADY *******

THOSE charms that time destroys the painter gives,
The beauty withers when the picture lives:
Be Shee your painter, but your poet I,
Verse lasts immortal, colours fade and die.
You, happy fair! perpetual bloom might hope
If Shee were Reynolds, and if I were Pope.

ARS LONGA, VITA BREVIS*.

Too fleeting life forbids us to be wise—
For, ere the sage is form'd, the mortal dies.

Trin. Coll. Camb.

* A saying of Hippocrates.

HORACE TO NEÆRA.

'TWAS night—the silver moon serenely shone,
The stars around her throne,
When you more close than clasping ivy twin'd
Within these arms reclin'd,
And swore by all the injur'd deities
These faithless perjuries:
" Long as the raging wolf the herd devours,
" Long as Orion pours
" His roaring tempest on the wintry wave
" To fright the sailor brave;
" Long as th' enamour'd wanton gale caresses
" Apollo's flowing tresses,
" Neæra's breast with mutual flames shall burn,
" And thy true love return."

Ah! cruel nymph, and shall thy Flaccns see
Another bless'd by thee?

Another swain enjoy his lost delights,

His happy, happy nights?

Ah! shall he see a rival's hated face

Contented with disgrace?

And you, fond boy! by my misfortune blest,

By my false fair carest;

Tho' in your wide domains Pactolus roll'd

His glittering sands of gold;

Tho' all the arts the sage of Samos knew

Belong'd alone to you;

Tho' your fair form e'en Nireus' form surpass'd,

Her love would never last;

Soon will her charms another swain beguile,

'Tis then that I shall smile.

Trin. Coll. Camb. 1805.

TRANSLATION FROM

COWLEY.

WHAT! verse again? O fool to feed once more
That dire disease that you so oft forswore;
That rooted ail that baffles all your skill,
Mocks force and reason yet, and ever will:
Does Jove, my friend, and all to favour you,
Laugh at the lover's lies, and poet's too?

Softly, good sir! forgive the son of song,
In rhyme's tight chains reluctant dragg'd along:
The doctor's art I lately dar'd to try,
And thought no dunce alive so calm as I;
But then, the moon at full has turu'd my brain,
And brought me my poetic fits again.

Trin. Coll. Camb.

HORACE, CARM. 28. III.

"Festo quid potiùs die," &c.

ODE FOR THE BIRTH-DAY. 1809.

FRIEND ——, since we both foresee
That certain folks must tumble soon,
How shall two jacobins agree
To celebrate the fourth of June?

At some French tavern let us dine
In spite of all the royal rout,
Two bottles of their oldest wine
Shall draw our rebel humours out.

Come, I will toast brave Clávering
And all the enemies of York,
Whilst you on t'other side shall sing
The deadly darts of Mrs. Clarke *.

* "Celeris spicula Cynthiæ."
The collector of these poems does not approve quite of the rhymes

Fair Anna! too resistless dame,
Whence every soldier sought promotion,
To whom each striving courtier came,
And churchmen too paid due devotion.

"Dear, pretty, darling girl!" for thee
Greenwood and Cox shall feel our spite;
But most, we'll drink in three times three,
Damnation to that scoundrel Knight *.

"York and Clarke," but the duke and the darling have been so often coupled together, that it would be a pity to part them in this place.

* Dicetur meritâ *Nox* quoque næniâ.

Trin. Coll. Camb. 1809.

ON

CHARLES FOX

BEING BURIED IN WESTMINSTER ABBEY, NEAR THE GRAVE OF

WILLIAM PITT.

YES, noble pair! Britannia's equal boast,
And rivals only who should serve her most;
One death unites you, and one grave contains
All that of man, of mighty man remains,
The mortal clay. Your souls together fly
To seek the mansions of your native sky,
And join the patriots in the realms above,
Who best deserv'd, and gain'd a nation's love;
For both to one great end your powers applied,
Both serv'd your country, and to save it—died.

F. Q.

ADDITIONAL LINES

AT THE CONCLUSION OF THE LAST BOOK OF ROWE'S LUCAN, WRITTEN BY

MRS. ROWE.

SOME looser Muse, perhaps, who lightly treads
The devious paths where wanton fancy leads,
In heaven's high court would feign the queen of Love,
Kneeling in tears before the throne of Jove;
Imploring sad th' Almighty Father's grace,
For the dear offspring of her Julian race:
While to the just recording Roman's eyes
Far different scenes and different gods arise.
The guardian furies round him rear their heads,
And Nemesis the shield of safety spreads;
Freedom and laws the Pharian darts withstand,
And save him for avenging Brutus' hand.

FEMALE LEVITY.

FROM Q CICERO.

Trust to the waves, but trust no woman's love,
For she less constant than the sea will prove;
No fair can faithful be, or if she should,
It shows a wondrous change from bad to good.

Trin. Coll. Camb. 1806.

A SIMILE FROM PLAUTUS.

How much a man is like a house!
My simile fits vastly close;
The structure first is fair and fine,
The work and workmen quite divine.
A tenant comes, for love of gain,
Shuts out the air, lets in the rain;

The rafters rot, the roofs decay,
And all the building falls away.
Thus following up the common plan,
Our parents strive to make a man;
They polish, teach, use constant care,
And no expense and labour spare.
'Twas thus with me whilst yet at home,
I dreamt not of my sins to come;
But when I left my friends' controul
And liv'd the master of my soul,
Then all my founder's care and cost,
And all their pains prov'd labour lost;
For sloth my tenant then became,
And shut the doors on sense and shame;
Let in the storm thro' every chink,
And left me what you see—a sink.

Trin. Coll. Camb.

AN

INSCRIPTION FOR THE BUST OF

VOLTAIRE.

WITH various parts for every effort fit,
With wisdom witty, and a sage with wit,
A hard, by every willing Muse belov'd,
By all but fools, and knaves, and kings approv'd,
Who superstition's idol durst despise,
And 'gainst the monster lift a mortal's eyes,
Thee, thee, Voltaire! exulting Gallia owns
The last and best of all her fav'rite sons.

Trin. Coll. Camb.

LADY *********

'Tis not her eyes, tho' Cupids ambush there,
'Tis not the beauties of her flowing hair;
'Tis not her breast, whose Parian hue might vie
With drifted snows on Etna's sides that lie;
And like those treach'rous snows would feign conceal
A warmth more genial which her eyes reveal;
But 'tis that winning, that resistless grace
Which moves her limbs and sparkles in her face;
Speaks in her voice, adorns and aids the whole,
Guide of her actions, offspring of her soul.

L. T.

LOVE DESPISED.

CAN any length of years gone by
Love's bliss destroy or ardour tame?
No, no: the passion that can die
Has ne'er deserv'd that blessed name.

Can brighter beauties e'er persuade
The lover from his fair to rove?
No, no: if any other maid
Seems fair to him, he does not love.

Can want, can woe, can misery blight
Sincere affection's impulse warm?
No: love is as the beacon's light,
Priz'd ever most amid the storm.

T. L.

TRANSLATED FROM CATULLUS.

TO CALVUS,

ON THE

DEATH OF QUINTILIA HIS WIFE.

If mortal sorrow on the silent dead
Calvus! can any touch of joy bestow,
When mourns regret o'er love for ever fled,
Or weeps for friendship it no more must know,

Oh! then Quintilia's spirit will not grieve
At early death and fate's unjust decree,
So much as she will gladden to perceive
How well, how truly, she was lov'd by thee.

T. L.

METASTASIO.

WHILST dreams and tales unreal I devise,
And strive to deck them with poetic art,
The self-sprung woes so touch my foolish heart,
I melt in anguish, and myself despise.

Haply, when snatch'd from fancy's blind controul,
Wisdom appears and calms my troubled soul;
Haply, I these impetuous transports prove
From the resistless influence of love.

Alas! not only these my mournful lays
Are fables all—whate'er I hope or fear,
Is all deceit, and life itself a maze,
A tedious, idle dream from year to year.
Grant me, O God! when the illusion's past,
Upon the breast of truth repose at last.

E. B.

DISAPPOINTMENT.

Ye fiends! from whose malignant hearts
All human evil erst began,
How weak would be your cruel arts,
The restless curses that ye plan;
The strokes and scourges poets feign
In vain you'd wield, and seek in vain
The misery of man;

Did not the powers of bliss provide
The source of greatest grief below;
Who scatter transient pleasures wide,
And joys that for a moment glow;
Which scarce have met our raptur'd gaze
Ere snatch'd away by you, they raise
Regret and keenest woe.

L. T.

TO

THE MEMORY OF A BRITISH OFFICER,

WHO WAS LOST IN THE ATHENIENNE, MAN OF WAR, FEB. 1807.

WHERE the rocks of Esquires* lie sunk in the wave
Have the billows engulph'd the unfortunate brave,
And cold o'er as gallant a bosom they flow,
As e'er felt for a friend or encounter'd a foe.

Poor Harry!—Tho' placid and smoothly may rest
The waves that lie heavy and chill on thy breast;
Tho' the depths of the ocean be calm and serene,
Nor a zephyr may ruffle its surface of green;
As wild as the wildest tornado that raves,
And uproots the huge sea from its bottomless caves;

* Commonly called "the Squills."

As the billows that madden'd in hurricanes foam,
Are the breasts of the friends that bewail thee at home.

But away with the pall and the hearse from my sight,
Not the gloom of the grave nor the silence of night,
Not the march of the funeral, solemn and slow,
Nor all ostentation of formaliz'd woe,
Is fitting, is able, to waken in me
One worthy, one just recollection of thee.
Not the slow-pealing organ or toll of the bell
Can inspire the sad friend who has known thee so well,
Who in youth and in pleasure with thee has sojourn'd,
To mourn for thee, Harry! as thou should'st be mourn'd.

Let the valiant with sympathy sigh at the name
Of the soldier who died in the outset to fame!
Let the gentle and mild by compassion be mov'd
For the grief of the many by whom thou wert lov'd!
How weak are the feelings that sympathy knows!
How false is the tear that from sentiment flows!

But strong are the silent regrets that depress
His breast, who in bliss and in rapture's excess,
In the highest enjoyments that life can unfold,
Still misses the friend that has stor'd them of old.

In the sports which so often have worn out the day,
At the banquet where thou wert the first of the gay;
In merriment's riot, in revelry's glare,
In the noise of the crowd, and the smiles of the fair;
'Tis there I shall mourn thee, there pensive and true
Will mem'ry those moments of friendship renew,
When youth offer'd pleasure alone as its scope,
And the present was bliss, and the future was hope;
When no thought could depress, and no caution reprove,
And all that we sought was wine, laughter, and love.

Nor ever again shall assemble in glee
The friends who so often have revell'd with thee;
The young and the thoughtless who folly adore,
The gay who have ne'er known reflection before;

But anon, they shall pause 'mid the fever of wine,
O'er some trait that's remember'd, some frolic of thine;
And mem'ry shall raise with lost pleasures imprest,
A smile on the cheek, with a sigh from the breast.
Then silent and sad as the fun'ral will be
The sound of the bumper devoted to thee;
And the feast be ennobled with feelings divine,
As the tears of the drinker are mix'd with his wine.

Then peace to thee, Harry!—As peacefully sleep
The dead in the storms and turmoil of the deep,
As they who in sorrow's magnificent gloom,
By the pomp of the funeral borne to the tomb,
(Man's latest and vainest effusion of pride)
Repose in the vault by their forefathers' side.

So peace to thee, Harry!—In pleasure and mirth
So often shall mem'ry recal thee to earth,
And fancy so oft in thy presence shall dwell,
'Twere falsehood to say, "Gallant Harry, farewell!"

T. L.

THE END.

T. Davison, Whitefriars,
London.

Lightning Source UK Ltd.
Milton Keynes UK
UKHW040736311218
334816UK00010B/476/P